ASSET-BASED REPRESENTATION

JORDAN WEISINGER, M.S., M.P.P.A., M.B.A.

DEDICATION

To all of the peaceful protesters that have failed
throughout history due to lack of support from their
implied leaders, elected and non-elected.

CONTENTS

ACKNOWLEDGMENTS

This book has identical content to "Democratic-Capitalism" which was released at the same time.

1 THE PROMISE

Discrimination is an enemy to all honest and equitable markets. It creates a permanent underclass of low paid workers and unprotected consumers where lower wage families are often forced to make hard decisions no reasonable person should have to make. Home ownership is out of reach for most when banks redline neighborhoods and deny bank loans to prospective borrowers. Business ownership is inherently riskier when banks refuse to give good terms on loans and consumers from the demographic-majority fear their neighborhoods too much to shop or diner at their storefronts. When graduates continue to suffer higher unemployment and lower wages even after securing a diploma, the value of education diminishes

Even the threat of incarceration loses its ability to discourage wrongdoing, if the risk of unemployment is high and when wages are so low, the only way to recover a middle-class lifestyle is through illicit incomes. When minorities are exceedingly victimized by over-policing, incarceration is priced into their cost benefit analyses evaluating the consequences of the behavior. If all rational actors in the economy used cost benefit analysis to measure out their behaviors, it is undeniable that poverty creates worse decisions when the consequences of those decisions are nearly indistinguishable from the average outcome for people in similar situations.

When persons with more family wealth and higher incomes make the same poor decisions, they often escape without consequences. They can apply for emergency loans to rescue businesses. They can afford quality lawyers avoiding the worst penalties of criminal behavior. Wealthy families can make the investments into education that poor families can't. There is the expectation of employment at higher wages, loans for business adventures, and more support from consumers. Every cost benefit analysis made by the establishment demographic-group excludes the more likely outcomes for minority groups, disregarding the experiences of a substantial portion of the public. They don't price in the same risks or the consequences, because they are less frequent and less severe, producing a lack of sympathy for minorities. The demographic-majority attributes the poor outcome to guiltiness and personal failure to rather than the systemic inequities and institutionalized racism.

Poverty is not an intrinsic property of the person but rather an artificial constraint on their natural abilities. Poverty is in their environment from the beginning. Their parents are in poverty, making a component of poverty learned. Their friends are in poverty, increase the risk of misbehavior and bad judgement being communicated by association. Their community businesses operate with small margins and lower profits, resulting in less hiring, more firing, and wages at the bare legal minimum. Their neighborhoods have less resources, less public goods, fewer opportunities. Societies can't expect every individual to use exceptional judgement when the environment is more hostile and institutions are less forgiving.

None of these expectations will be met when so much of the poverty is due to discrimination; a legacy of hatred and exploitation that persists over generations. High unemployment rates in minority populations demonstrate discrimination by business owners and hiring managers. Lower median household incomes in minority populations demonstrate explicit exploitation by industries that do hire them. All of these statistics demonstrate a theme of exclusion. The same people coming to racists conclusions are making the wage and employment decisions justifying the belief. It's a tautology that preserves an unjust criminal justice system and an unequal economy. Many exceptional persons born into poverty, climb out of poverty, but this is far from expected in average cases. Many more persons will stay in poverty, trapped in a cycle of low wage labor, health crises, legal issues, and other problems. It is the average outcome that is important when determining public policy, not the far less likely exceptional outcome.

Discrimination concentrates wealth and power in the establishment demographic group. Consequently, the establishment demographic group won't have the same life experiences or economic expectations as the discriminated-against minority groups. They will form different political parties and support radically different public policies, dividing the nation around very discrete racial boundaries or economic preferences. The demographic-majority group will abuse firm power and due process to preserve wealth and insulating their behaviors from oversight and accountability. These sectarian differences foster a culture where labor is cheap, life is disposable, and where maintaining a monopoly on political power is the only way to attain permanent security for themselves or their families.

Racism is coded into public policy by pursuing a low tax, deregulated, and over-policed society where a wicked party cam prey on the ignorance and negligence of the public. The establishment party purposefully confounds poverty with race in order to preserve their superior economic position and political power; discrimination makes the two less distinguishable. They use coded language to escape the consequences of judgment while still enforcing harsh economic conditions and mass incarceration to preserve their wealth and electoral advantages. The establishment party will resist all anti-discrimination policies out of fear it will result in their children, friends, family, and neighbors losing their jobs, facing lower wages, and higher incarceration rates.

Few democratic nations can persist in an environment of concealed racism. Coded language in public policy allows racism to be institutionalized in the culture and law, without accepting credit for the abuse. As the wealth inequality exacerbates, corruption will permeate every aspect of the political process, tensions will mount, and it will be conceivable that every election will result in a catastrophic end to the democracy. Political parties will rely on legislative obstruction to limit government interference in their profiteering and abuse. They will pursue anti-democratic policies allowing them to control electoral outcomes and limit oversight by an opposition party. Only a fundamentalist capitalist nation will remain, with the establishment demographic group in firm control of the legal system and economy, perpetuating a low tax and deregulated state they can easily disregard.

One of the most important characteristics of Democratic-Capitalism is its anti-discriminatory properties. For the first time in the history, the consequences of racism and poorly managed economy will have a direct impact on public policy by providing a countervailing force through improved minority representation. When a demographic group suffers employment and wage discrimination, they will gain representational advantages in the legislature, proportional to the severity of the prejudice. When discrimination is present, the affected demographic groups will be concentrated in one of the two bicameral chambers, allowing them to use collective bargaining and majority power within the institution to achieve reforms that will mitigate the exploitation.

When economic inequalities persist, Asset-based representation concentrates minorities in a single legislative chamber, allowing them to protect their economic rights and civil rights through chairing committees and using embargos on corporate subsidies and tax laws. With a majority in one chamber of a bicameral legislature, they can use market power to defeat bills promoting voter suppression through mass incarceration, voter ID laws, voter registration purges, gerrymandering, and deregulated private campaign laws. If the demographic-majority wants to pass any tax breaks, defense spending, corporate subsidies, or any trade bills they will have to first negotiate and compromise on labor rights, voting rights, and civil rights bills coming from the non-owners chamber. Nothing will move in the legislature without the implied consent of the governed, focusing on the interests of minorities.

A coalition of minorities only need 51% of the non-owner chamber to exert majority control over the chamber. Having a 51% majority in the non-owner chamber allows them to block all legislation production in the bicameral process, block appointments to cabinets and senior leadership positions, intervene with oversight hearings, and it gives them a public platform to coordinate general strikes and government shutdowns. The demographic-majority and wealthy elites will be forced to negotiate labor rights, civil rights, and voting rights with them or risk losing access to federal subsidies and the protection of federal law enforcement. No legislation will pass through the bicameral process until concessions are made to minority groups.

When minority groups are concentrated in one of the chambers, it gives them a much stronger position within the party. A minority group only needs a 26% share of seats in the chamber to effectively control the institution when their party is in the majority. With slightly more than one-third of the seats in the chamber, they can exert influence over their own party and dictate agendas. They can more aggressively negotiate with their own party, giving them more opportunities to acquire appointments to important committees with more senior leadership roles. As the minority population grows, they will assume an increasingly larger share of the seats in the chamber, making it more likely they acquire 26% or 51% majorities. If the discrimination goes unchecked, the coalition will eventually exert monopoly control over the party and chamber.

When there is no discrimination present in the economy, minority groups are likely to be evenly distributed among the two legislative chambers, giving them proportional representation to the majority-demographic group. If during this arrangement, anti-discrimination laws are passed and enforced, preserving a competitive economy, the minority coalition won't benefit from any improved representation. As long there are no differences in income, unemployment, and home ownership, minority groups won't be concentration in the non-owners chamber. Harmony is preserved for as long as the promise is of equality is delivered.

Democratic-Capitalism is an ideal system of government due specifically to its ability to minimize the risks systemic racism poses to competitive labor, real estate, and political markets. The expectations are that a free market economy provides the highest living standard possible at the time, while honest and accurate elections promote public policy mitigating the deficiencies inherent in inflexible commodities and other market failures. Racism interferes with the government's ability to identify social or economic issues and respond quickly by passing laws and overcoming financial crises, wars, and political abuses. Racism also results in voter suppression efforts, mass incarceration, and other anti-democratic policies like deregulated campaign finance, making elections an inaccurate reflection of the current political market. Without honest and accurate elections, no equity is delivered to the public and economic markets will fail. If the nation can't secure for itself free and fair elections, the public won't have any trust in its democratic institutions and public policy.

Competitive markets are the life sustaining force for all nations. A compromise in one will invariably start to break down the other. Capitalist economy requires transparent transactions between sellers and buyers. Democracy requires transparent transactions between constituents and elected officials. Flawed political markets produce more unequal economies, begging for a correction in both. In exploitative capitalist economies a correction could mean a permanent loss of GDP or living standards, while corrections in democracy could result despotism or communism. Inaccurate elections and weak institutions will foster more extreme outcomes in the political markets, resulting in a positive feedback loop to a collapse in both economy and civil society.

If the middle class is unable to intervene in the political markets with the necessary numerical superiority to outweigh the economic power of the elite and industrialists, there will be no reform of the economy, concentrating both power and wealth within the owners class. Radicalism will root in the electorate, making reform less likely. In illiberal democracies, federal and state governments will be perpetually under-funded, industries will be deregulated, firms will start to rival states, and the owners class will dominant the political process.

In adequately regulated and taxed economies, voters will be more moderate and tolerant of sectarian differences. When more equal economic outcomes are achieved, the electorate makes better decisions. They elect sounder politicians and support more reasonable policies on wages, taxes, and civil rights. Tolerant positions can't be preserved long if discrimination is present and the industrialists can inculcate a culture of exploitation and racial inequality. Hatred will be taught, allowing industrialists to easily divide and distract the electorates.

Democratic-Capitalism compensates the oppressed and exploited with more representation in the bicameral legislative process where they can better defend themselves. This is the promise, but minority groups can't simply rely on the goodness of the majority-demographic group to grant them civil rights and voting rights. Due process often fails to yield productive results when minority groups and opposition parties pursue reforms. Minority groups must be more than just stakeholders, they must be active participants. When reform movements falter, their citizens can turn to institutional protests to recapture the promise of democracy. Government shutdowns, debt defaults, and tax protests are important strategies that can provide recourse when the political markets fail to provide honest and accurate elections. They are all nonviolent and depend on the laws found in most federal systems. Institutional protests are inherently lawful and give political parties, an opportunity to cure defects in leadership, without relying on individuals or state sanctioned violence.

Institutional protests may be the best strategy minority groups and their allies have to push for reforms remaking the government more in their image. When the public stirs dissent and mobilizes for change, their elected leaders must demonstrate support and commitment to the cause. Promises are not enough. Politicians must repay their constituents by supporting them with government shutdowns, debt defaults, or tax protests. Outcomes are the only measure of success, and this requires fealty from politicians to their constituents. Rhetoric is not enough. There must be consequences to systemic abuses and illegitimate force. Reform must be sought under the aegis of institutional protests.

2 FOUNDATIONS OF POWER

Property Ownership has long denoted political power. Before there were contemporary democracies, most nations were ruled by monarchs and aristocracies that predicated their power on land ownership. Feudal governments throughout Europe persisted for hundreds of years. Even the ancient Roman republics had aspects of wealth deeply intertwined within their political structures[1]. Most of these systems were exclusionary. Property owners controlled all aspects of the political process and denied voting rights and civil liberties to all nonowners. To own land was the most significant economic and political goal a person or family could achieve. However, for most people, it was an unattainable dream; they were excluded due to race, gender, or class. Structural inequality rendered all Asset-based systems of representation immoral and elitist, despite preserving legal and political authority.

Now, there are expectations of universal suffrage with unfettered access to voting regardless of demographic characteristics. Democracies are measured by their ability to deliver equal and proportional representation, with each person getting exactly one vote. This concept is incompatible with prior iterations of Asset-based representation. No contemporary democracies have land requirements, but with

---

[1] Donald L. Wasson, "Roman Republic," Ancient History Encyclopedia, April 07, 2016, retrieved from https://www.ancient.eu/Roman_Republic/.

modest reforms, Asset-based representation can be transformed into one of the highest-quality forms of democracy. With powerful anti-discrimination properties, Asset-based representation elevates itself above more conventional forms of democracy, making it a superior choice for reformers and nation-builders.

There are a few methods for how home ownership can be used to deliver representation to the citizens of a nation. The first and most prominent way uses a binary partition to split the electorate into two unequal parts, with homeowners voting in one chamber and non-owners voting in the other chamber. The second-best method uses a median partition, based on either property values or ownership rates, to split the public into two equal parts. Districts or states are ranked in order from least to greatest and separated, with one group voting in the below median chamber and the other group voting in the above median chamber. The third method uses a representational coefficient determined by multiplying median property values by population. Coefficients are derivative of both wealth and demographics, producing a foil to more conventional chambers used un bicameral legislatures.

In micropolitical systems, individuals are segregated by personal ownership status; the entire electorate is split by the binary of ownership, with homeowners voting in one chamber and non-owners voting in the other. The number of representations apportioned to each state depends on the proportional size of their population. Universal suffrage applies with all eligible voters being assigned to either one chamber or the other. Binary partitions rely on a more discrete relationship between representatives and their constituents, while preserving the high standard of majority rule with a demographic-based representational coefficient.

Within micropolitical binary partitions, there is a more adversarial relationship between the homeowners class and the non-owners class. The benefits of one class often comes at the expense of the other. Micropolitical partitions create value in the electorate by segregating the two parts in separate institutions, the same way specialization in the division of labor within a production line creates value. When the voter identifies as one class or the other, the bonds between members of an electorate become stronger. They share role identity, financial interests, and institutional familiarity.

Class tensions are a dominant theme in the cannon of political discourse and economics. It always has been and always will be an eternal struggle between "haves", "have-nots", and everybody in between. Vibrant electorates contain persons from every class, trade, religion, race, and gender. It is expected that the competing political parties can negotiate on the nuances of public policy by appealing to moderates who may have occupied multiple roles and classes during their lifetime. Contemporary democracies are made of special interest groups and diverse demographics that lend to more bartering between the candidates and parties.

Most of history describes an unending struggle where the underclass grinds out incremental reforms. Asset-based representation will be an accelerant to the process. Homogeneity in the owners class makes them much more predictable. When these incentives can be identified, they can be used by the non-owners class to barter concessions and reforms. If the owners class wants a particular reform, they can seek out a special interest group to align with and pass the measure. When the predictability of the owners class is reconciled with the diversity of the non-owners class, reforms can be achieved that promote greater equity and more class mobility between the two classes.

In micropolitical partitions, the negotiated benefits can be measured in terms of precise costs and the time it takes to acquire the benefit. The time value of money is a powerful concept during the barter for reform; the difference in rents and incomes between classes can be evaluated and compared to the revenues of firms or wealth of families. More importantly, when discrimination is present in the economy, minorities will have separate and unequal outcomes when compared to the demographic-majority, changing the calculus in policy preferences found within the legislatures. These differences aren't only priced into the electoral outcomes allocating political power, it is baked into the very structure of the political process by increasing the influence of the minority groups facing discrimination.

Wealth is often accumulated through abuse of monopoly, political power, and a host of other deficiencies in capitalist markets and inefficient democracies. Wealthier populations have always pursued public policies that preserved their wealth or multiplied it the expense of the underclass, creating economic conditions that invite reform. They are so low in equity that they can only be bargained upward. When the nation lacks adequate minimum wage laws, labor rights, and consumer protections, everything negotiated looks like a major improvement in station and opportunity. In this environment, the non-owners class is more likely to participate in general strikes and institutional protests when the owners class reluctant to negotiate. If all of the economic benefit goes to the landowners and firm owners, there is less risk for the underclass to disrupt ordinary commerce when bartering and negotiating for reforms.

When homeowners are separated from non-owners, it engenders more role identity into the two chambers representing the constituencies. Non-owners will vote in separate elections from homeowners, allowing them to cultivate elected officers who better represent their interests. Any representative wishing to earn election or reelection will have to advocate for policies that exclusively benefit the non-owner electorate. They can drill down and focus on rental protections, fairer eviction laws, more equitable urban planning, and civil rights for non-owners. They can also find representatives that resemble them in income, race, gender, and education, providing a huge advantage over conventional demographic-based democracies which often result in homogenous electoral outcomes favoring the establishment demographic group. To the benefit of the nation, the non-owner electorate will be incredibly diverse, including wealthy urbanites, rural laborers, and young office workers.

Identity politics is a critical element of Democratic-Capitalism. It is expected that the interests of students and pensioners are different from those of landlords and firm owners. This is necessary for the political markets to price in the supply of opportunity with the demand for satisfaction. The agents for the classes can compare the costs of concession to the risks of tolerating abusive or exploitative behavior. Each agent will share similar economic interests with their constituents making them more suitable to defend their rights. Most reforms require barter and compromise to achieve. Democratic-Capitalism aids this process by intertwining economic output with political power. When inequalities surface in the economy, they will eventually be expressed within the political process.

Home ownership is not like an identity based on income. A median income, including non-income earners, splits the population into two equal parts. With Homeownership, two distinct but unequal populations are created. Unlike Income-based representation, home ownership doesn't imply any thresholds on value. Homeowners of small and inexpensive properties are just as qualified as homeowners of middle class or luxury homes. Home ownership isn't naturally based on gender or race unless discrimination is present. These characteristics potentiate home ownership as an equalizing force between members of an electorate. Considering the innate, homeownership is one of the best strategies to divide electorate into two co-equal chambers of a single bicameral legislature.

Homeownership is fungible. Over the course of a lifetime, one can be renter, homeowner, and landlord. It is an attribute that is found outside of oneself, one's employment, and one's residency. Homeownership is also transitory. If the citizens of the nation see more benefits to ownership, they can attempt to buy property, if they see more benefits to renting, they can sell the property, producing a market vectorized with political identity. The market economy is natural protections against one status being too heavily favored by voters. When one electorate grows in size, the other shrinks impacting representational ratios between the two chambers. A smaller electorate will still control half of the number of representatives and half of the bicameral process, allowing them to exert more individual influence over the political process.

This imbalance in representational ratios between the two chambers sets up non-monetary incentives for acquiring home ownership or preferring renting. If there are more homeowners than renters, renters will have an advantage in representation to accommodate for their lack of ownership. Voters who value political influence more than monetary rewards can adapt their behavior to maximize their returns. Binary partitions are remarkable in that they can add value to both renting and homeownership by virtue of the extra representation earned or lost. Supply and demand will continue to dictate prices, while political preferences are in play on the margins.

One of the more interesting properties of econometric systems of representation, is that the state or federal government can intervene with public policy to correct market failures affecting the political process. The fear is that homeowners will monopolize the ownership chamber by escalating home values and pricing out a majority of the public. If there are fewer homeowners than expected, local and state governments can step in and provide more affordable housing to equalize the size of the electorates. Non-owners will be able to negotiate for reforms by embargoing tax subsidies and trade deals until more housing units are built. Smaller owners classes, risk losing the support of the military and police if concessions are not made, increasing the threat of more aggressive wealth distribution if equitable public policy is not passed.

Micropolitical binary partitions permit eligibility constraints to be imposed on candidates for office within the chambers. Any person can be excluded from running for office in the non-owners chamber if they or a family member owns property. This isn't as strong a constraint as income limits, but it does ensure some similarities in class identity. All candidates will all have relationships with landlords, concerns with leases, issues with maintenance, and have similar expectations for economic reforms within the real estate market. Not all rents are equal, but all candidates will come from the communities where the districts are located, creating a tendency for candidates to have more similar incomes as their constituents.

In many respects, an eligibility constraint related to home ownership is much sounder than an eligibility constraint by income. Income constraints place limits on how much the candidates can earn while in office, discouraging many of the older, more education, more successful, or more entrepreneurial citizens from running for office. This isn't true for property owners. Renters can be high-wage earners as well as low wage earners. In expensive cities, any demographic, educational, or professional attribute can describe a renter. The candidate can have any professional experience, any income, any education, be of any gender or race, and still qualify with a status of homeowner or renter. This diversity is often impossible in other econometric systems of representation.

When nations are organized around macropolitical median partitions, states or districts are ranked in order from the lowest ownership rates to highest ownership rates and split by the median percentage of ownership. Jurisdictions with below median rates of ownership are placed within one chamber and jurisdictions with above median rates of ownership are placed in the other chamber. Although macropolitical partitions have less cohesion between voters in the electorates, they manufacture sounder representational ratios when the population is split into two equally sized groups.

Macropolitical methods produce more diverse electorates than micropolitical methods. A micropolitical binary partition will allocate each person to a chamber, regardless of their residency. Thus, public policy can be targeted specifically to non-owners or owners depending on the party designing the bill. Macropolitical median partitions aggregate constituents around districts or states, regardless of personal ownership status, forcing political parties have to design public policy that accommodates the interests of both owners and nonowners. The intermingling the wealthy and poor in the same district and chamber will produce more moderate parties and policies.

Macropolitical partitions can also use median home values to determine the allocation of jurisdictions to the below median chamber and above median chamber. Using home values imparts a powerful class identity into the bicameral process, capturing the best characteristics of Income-based representation while still relying on aggregated electorates. Poor districts are will work with other poor districts to pass laws ameliorating lower wages, crime, and other defects in capitalist economy. Wealthier districts will organize themselves for sounder public finance, investments into commercial infrastructure, subsidies in innovative technologies, and other aspects of good governance. The diverse electorates will ensure competitive elections keep the parties honest despite the strong cultural under-currents in the institutions.

Most contemporary democracies use senates which degrade the quality of representation by over-representing lower populated, poorer, less educated, and more rural states. Macropolitical representation provides universal suffrage with a bicameral legislature based entirely on demographic-based representation. Macropolitical systems marry proportional representation to the checks and balances of a bicameral chamber. New nations can have the safety of a bicameral process, with the equity of a straight proportional representation system. Not only will all eligible persons have the right to vote but their votes will have equal in influence.

A more traditional Asset-based representation coefficient is based on a state's median property value multiplied by the population[2]. Value coefficients are a form a wealth-based representation rather than class-based representation. The states with the largest populations and highest property values will acquire the most representatives. The states with the lowest property values and the smallest population, will gain the least seats within the chamber. Historically, most wealth-based systems of representation relied on appointments and legacy, but now the offices can be elected, with the benefits of political power going to the community rather than individuals.

When econometric values are used to determine representation, there is a reciprocal relationship between a political system and its economy. It is public policy that determines tax policies, minimum wages, standards, best practices, and a host of other economic conditions which directly impact economic output. When econometric-based

---

[2] (state's property value x population)/ (nation's property value x population/ number of seats in chamber)

representational coefficients are used, it results in a more balanced equation, where economic output determines representation, representation determines public policy, and public policy shapes the environment where firms and individuals compete. Politics and economy were once considered the same field. With Democratic-Capitalism, the two will be unified again when economic output determines representation within the legislative branch.

Asset-based representational coefficients can be adjusted by multiplying the first figure by the proportion of home ownership in the state. This equalization factor is based exclusively on public policy and can be changed irrespective of the demographic or economic composition of the state. One of the biggest advantages this form of government has, is local and state governments can increase their own number of representatives by passing laws that make it easier to own properties and reduce the numbers of homeless persons. States will have incentives to distribute affordable housing to their residents when it increases the number of representatives sitting in the federal legislature, bringing down the value of other properties but improving the ratio of property owners. A higher ownership percentage converts more of the property value to seats in the legislative chamber.

When Asset-based representation is used as a representational coefficient, it offers an opportunity to deviate from demographic systems relying on numerical superiority diffusing the fear and anxiety of population changes and their impact on electoral outcomes, without fully decoupling from majority rule. Value coefficients are derivative of both population and median property values, so wealthier states have more representatives and higher populous states more representatives. Using both inputs, changes the representation coefficient enough to assuage the concerns of populism in a purely demographic-based system, while still respecting the tenants of majority rule and universal suffrage.

3 APPLIED OUTCOMES

The presence of discrimination is the world is undeniable. It is also nearly unshakeable. Once it roots in a political system and culture, it becomes resistant to the reform movements and laws that should otherwise mitigate the problem. At least until now. Democracy has the power to change itself; to alter its own form in response to environmental stimulus and overcome those obstacles or deficiencies. Democracy is more than just a complex set of precepts and procedural tools; it is a living breathing organism able to overcome most obstacles with its own diversity and self-interests. Democracy evolves by constantly re-organizing itself with new laws, new public policy, and new amendments to meet the peoples' demands for security and equity.

Econometric systems of representation are a major evolutionary step in democratic theory. Contemporary versions of democracy have the anti-discriminatory properties found in income, tax, or Asset-based systems of representation. When discrimination is present in the economy, minorities will see a proportional increase in the quality of their representation. When the discrimination ends, their representation falls back to levels equivalent to traditional demographic representation. The longer political parties resist reform mitigating discrimination, the longer oppressed minority groups have improved representation and oversight over the government. The worse the discrimination, the more likely minority groups gain majority control over legislative institutions within the government. Empowering minorities through representation is the absolute best method to avoid conflict and violence; it is only through due process that real racial equality can be achieved. Incremental reform is the most certain and safest way to achieve all of the necessary changes to perfect a union and distribute equity to the entire electorate.

The best example for this anti-discriminatory property is the United States. The U.S. has had endemic and systemic racism for hundreds of years, resulting is minorities underperforming in home ownership in a country that heavily incentivizes the behavior. If discrimination was not present, the rates of home ownership for African Americans and Hispanics would be equal to that of the Caucasian population. They are not. Neither are median incomes, educational attainment, or other indicators of economic success. How different would the United States be if they had an Asset-based system of representation? The answer is simple. Minorities would have nearly double the proportional representation within the non-owners chamber, and therefore would be able to more quickly achieve economic parity through anti-discrimination laws, better labor rights, and stronger voting rights.

If one looks at the United States as a model for Income-based representation, African Americans and Native Americans would see an average of 27% improvement in representation, while Hispanics would benefit from a 13% improvement. Although their representative in the below median chamber is increased, they wouldn't acquire a majority until after 2045[3]. If one looks at the United States as a model for Asset-based representation, a coalition of minorities would have earned a 51% majority in the non-owners chamber by 2020[4], delivering on the promise of majority power nearly twenty-five years ahead of the demographic shift and income or Tax-based econometric systems of representation.

The first set of simulations examine the United States using a micropolitical method for allocating constituents.

---

[3] Jordan Weisinger, "Income-based Representation", South Carolina: Kindle Direct Publishing, 2019, pp. 27.
[4] Table 1.14 2020 Micropolitical Demographics and Ownership

Census data from 2000 and Census projections for 2020 and 2030 are used in conjunction with homeownership numbers to estimate the disposition of seats within the binary partition chambers. None of the demographic data cited contains Native American, Native Alaskans, Native Hawaiian, and Pacific Islanders, but the simulation still provides a good generalized estimate of what the binary partition would look like after years of demographic growth in the minority populations.

There is another caveat; the party breakdown of demographic groups is not treated within the simulation, so any estimates of electoral outcomes are not offered. Nearly 39% of the Caucasian population voters support liberal or progressive candidates but these simulations don't tease out a combined plurality that predicts a party's performance during elections[5]. Hispanics, like Caucasians are not monolithic is their political preferences. In recent years they have been split 63% to 37% by party[6]. African Americans favor the liberal candidates by a margin of 83% to 17%[7]. Asians prefer more liberal candidates by a margin on 72% to 28%[8]. Most of the estimates disregard the party preference based on race to focus on gross minority representation in the representational system.

Looking at ownership rates and demographic data for 2000, there is substantial improvement in representation for minorities when using Asset-based representation rather than a conventional demographic-based system. Asset-based

---

[5] Joshua Zingher, "Whites have fled the Democratic Party. Here's how the nation got there.", The Washington Post, May 22, 2018, retrieved from https://www.washingtonpost.com/news/monkey-cage/wp/2018/05/22/whites-have-fled-the-democratic-party-heres-how-the-nation-got-there/

[6] Pew Research Center, "U.S. Politics & Policy", Pew Research Center, June 2, 2020, page 3, retrieved from https://www.pewresearch.org/politics/2020/06/02/democratic-edge-in-party-identification-narrows-slightly/

[7] Pew Research Center, "U.S. Politics & Policy", Pew Research Center, June 2, 2020, page 3, retrieved from https://www.pewresearch.org/politics/2020/06/02/democratic-edge-in-party-identification-narrows-slightly/

[8] Pew Research Center, "U.S. Politics & Policy", Pew Research Center, June 2, 2020, page 3, retrieved from https://www.pewresearch.org/politics/2020/06/02/democratic-edge-in-party-identification-narrows-slightly/

representation provides a roughly 50% improvement in representation for minority groups in the non-owners chamber[9]. Collectively, African Americans, Hispanics, and Asians would command more than 46% of the seats in the non-owners chamber[10]. This is a significant increase over the approximate 29% share of representation expected in a traditional demographic-based chamber[11]. With 46% of all seats in the chamber, minorities could demand more voting rights, labor rights, and anti-discrimination laws, while negotiating ordinary budget appropriations and international trade agreements.

In 2000, Caucasians were 69% of the population with 72.5% qualifying as homeowners[12], translating to 78 % of the seats in the ownership chamber and 55% of the seats in the non-owners chamber[13]. African Americans were 12.9% of the population with only 46.3% qualifying as homeowners[14]. As a result, African Americans would occupy roughly 9% of the seats in the ownership chamber and nearly 20% of the seats in the non-ownership chamber[15]. The concentration of African Americans in the non-owners chamber improves their net representation by more than 54%. Asian Americans were just 4.2% of the population with only 53% qualifying as homeowners, resulting in control of 3.0% of the seats in the ownership chamber and nearly 6% of the seats in the non-owners chamber[16]. For Asian Americans, there was a slight loss of representation in the owners chamber but that is offset by a small gain in representation within the non-owners chamber. Hispanic Americans were 12.5% of the population, with a homeownership rate of only 46%[17], resulting in control of nearly 9% of the seats in the owners chamber and nearly 20% in the non-owners chamber[18]. Hispanic Americans would

---

9 Table 1.13 2000 Micropolitical Demographics and Ownership
10 Table 1.13 2000 Micropolitical Demographrics and Ownership
11 Table 1.13 2000 Micropolitical Demographics and Ownership
12 Table 1.13 2000 Micropolitical Demographics and Ownership
13 Table 1.13 2000 Micropolitical Demographics and Onwership
14 Table 1.13 2000 Micropolitical Demographics and Ownership
15 Table 1.13 2000 Micropolitical Demographics and Ownership
16 Table 1.13 2000 Micropolitical Demographics and Ownership
17 Table 1.13 2000 Micropolitical Demographics and Ownership
18 Table 1.13 2000 Micropolitical Demographics and Ownership

have seen the nearly same gains (54%) as African Americans in the non-owners chamber.

Working together, the three minority groups acquire more than 46% of the seats in the non-owners chamber, giving them a near majority, and suffering only a modest reduction in representation within the owners chamber. Combined, African American, Hispanics, and Asians had nearly 22% of seats in the owners class which is only a slight reduction from the 29% expected[19]. This 22% is not enough to acquire the 26% needed for majority control over a party in the chamber, but it should still impart significant influence over agendas in the owners chamber. The nearly 8% loss in the ownership chamber is more than compensated for by the nearly 16% increase in the non-owners chamber[20].

When the minority groups lose 8% of their seats in the owners chamber, Caucasians see a 16% gain in the proportion of seats. However, as the majority-demographic group, they already had a commanding majority in all chambers using demographic-based representational coefficients. If Caucasians accounted for 69% of the population, they should have 69% of the seats in both chambers, producing no additional value. A 78% majority does not provide more political power than a 69% majority. The same is not true for a minority group that see their control of seats grow from 29% to over 46%. Acquiring more seats in a chamber a demographic-majority already have a majority in, is worth less political and social capital than minority groups gaining a near majority in a chamber where they previously had only slightly less than 30% minority share.

With Asset-based representation, minority populations would have more leadership positions on legislative committees, be able to use collective bargaining and leverage within their own party to acquire more reforms and demand more oversight on consumer and regulatory affairs. With 46% of the seats in the non-owners chamber, the issues that matter most to the minority population will become the issues that mattered most to the country. No bills will pass through the

---

[19] Table 1.13 2000 Micropolitical Demographics and Ownership
[20] Table 1.13 2000 Micropolitical Demographics and Ownership

bicameral legislature until criminal justice reforms, voter registration reforms, minimum wage and union reforms are negotiated.

As time passes, the situation would improve for minority voters. By 2020, Caucasians are expected to be just 60.1% of the total population with 73.2% classified as property owners[21]. They would still control nearly 71.5% of all seats in the owners chamber but only slightly more than 45.3% of the non-owners chamber[22]. African Americans will make up more than 13.4% of the population with home ownership just 41.5%[23]. As a result, African Americans would likely control slightly more than 9.0% of seats in the owners chamber and approximately 19.6% of the non-owners chamber[24]. Asian Americans grow to 5.9% of the total population with ownership rates of 53.4%[25], providing control of 5.1% of owners chamber and more than 7.5% of the non-owners chamber[26]. Hispanic Americans grow to 18.5% of the population and with just 47.3% homeownership[27], they can expect to control over 14.2% of the owners chamber and 27.5% of the non-ownership chamber[28]. Together, Asian Americans, African Americans, and Hispanics will occupy close to a 55% in the non-owners chamber.

2020 marks the year and first time when African Americans, Asians, and Hispanics gain a majority in the non-owners chamber. It's not a strong majority, just barely more than 50%, but it should be large enough, when combined with political allies in the Caucasian population, to routinely dictate policy in legislative process[29]. The predictable majority the non-owners chamber will give minority-demographic groups a permanent platform to lobby the public and stakeholders for reform. They will now be able to lead negotiations for laws prohibiting and ameliorating discrimination by leveraging an

---

[21] Table 1.14 2020 Micropolitical Demographics and Ownership
[22] Table 1.14 2020 Micropolitical Demographics and Ownership
[23] Table 1.14 2020 Micropolitical Demographics and Ownership
[24] Table 1.14 2020 Micropolitical Demographics and Ownership
[25] Table 1.14 2020 Micropolitical Demographics and Ownership
[26] Table 1.14 2020 Micropolitical Demographics and Ownership
[27] Table 1.14 2020 Micropolitical Demographics and Ownership
[28] Table 1.14 2020 Micropolitical Demographics and Ownership
[29] Table 1.14 2020 Micropolitical Demographics and Ownership

embargo dependent exclusively on their own electoral performance. As the majority-party, they would be able to leverage their oversight over executive agencies to pursue anti-discriminatory public policy even when they can't pass the measures through the bicameral legislature.

Most of the focus is on achieving at least a 55% majority but minority groups will still benefit tremendously when they are in much smaller proportions. A minority group, with 26% of the seats in one chamber, has a strong enough position to dictate conditions within their own party. The same principles that apply when gaining a majority in the chamber, apply when minority groups gain a majority in party seats. A political party won't be able to pass any laws without explicit cooperation from the minority groups. If the minority groups hold more that 26% of the chambers seats, they can set the policy agendas and demand more chairperson roles on committees. They will be able to leverage their newfound majority power within the institution into leadership positions within the party.

Make no mistake, a 26% margin it is nowhere near as influential as managing a 55% margin in the chamber, but if it helps to ameliorate wage and hiring discrimination a decade or two before a majority is achieved, it would be worth converting to an Asset-based system of representation. Collective bargaining was responsible for most of the concessions earned by employees and consumers over the last 100 years. An Asset-based system of representation extends these negotiating strategies into the political realm. It makes collective bargaining a permanent aspect of negotiating roles within the political parties and bartering for reforms with the opposition party. When there are structural reforms that distribute political power to minorities, it changes both what is possible and what is expected. Only when the culture is changed, can minorities expect rational economic and legal outcomes.

By 2030, the African American populations will grow to 13.8% of the population and if they maintain the 41.5% ownership rate, they will control nearly 9.5% of the owners chamber and nearly 20.3% of the non-owners chamber[30].Asian

Americans will grow to about 6.9% of the population. If they maintain their 53.4% ownership rate, they will manage nearly 6.1% of the owners chamber and 8.8% of the non-owners chamber[31]. By 2030, the Hispanic population will acquire nearly 21% of the total population, and with a 47.3% ownership rate, they will control nearly 16.5% of the owners chamber and more than 31.2% of the non-owners chamber[32].

By 2030, the growth experienced in the minority populations over ten years results in a solid 60% majority in the non-owners chamber and a 29% minority in the owners class[33]. This 60% margin includes no mandatory participation by sympathetic Caucasians. Not only will minority have an explicit institutional majority in the non-owners chamber, but they will have a majority in the owners chamber when working with Caucasians within their own party. When the minority population works with political allies within the Caucasian demographic group, they could predictably achieve a majority in the owners chamber while maintaining a 60% margin in the non-owners chamber[34].

The next simulation examines Asset-based representation usefulness during reconstruction periods. If the Southern States were to attempt to secede again and fail, it would give the Northern states an opportunity to remake them on the state-level. It would require a period of occupation, but it may be the very best and last opportunity for the nation to ensure the South remains democratic and part of the union. Peace can only be guaranteed when there are free and fair elections in the South, resulting in more diversity in representation and higher quality candidates.

One of the reasons the Republican party has been so dominant in federal elections is that they can control the electoral outputs with anti-democratic policies passed on the state level. If the democratic states can't guarantee honest and accurate election on the state-level within the South, the federal electoral output will remain fixed and easily

---

[30] Table 1.15 2030 Micropolitical Demographics and Ownership
[31] Table 1.15 2030 Micropolitical Demographics and Ownership
[32] Table 1.15 2030 Micropolitical Demographics and Ownership
[33] Table 1.15 2030 Micropolitical Demographics and Ownership
[34] Table 1.15 2030 Micropolitical Demographics and Ownership

exploitable by future authoritarians. If the South can continue to control their own electoral output by voter suppression and mass incarceration, they will continue to threaten democracy on the federal level. Only Asset-based representation can deliver outcomes that will make it impossible for the Southern states to organize another rebellion.

When Asset-based representation is installed within the Southern States during Reconstruction, 7 of the 12 states will deliver majority power to a coalition of African Americans, Asians, Hispanics, and Native Americans[35] within the non-owners chamber. Alabama will set aside 52% of seats in the non-owners chamber for minorities. Mississippi will set aside 61% of seats, South Carolina 54%, North Carolina 55%, Georgia 62%, Florida 64%, and Texas 74%[36]. With majority power in the non-owners chamber, minorities can effectively obstruct all voter ID laws, prevent voter roll purges, investigate all polling place closures, and take the necessary actions to protect their voting rights.

Within the owners chamber, a coalition of minorities exceeds the 26% threshold in 6 of the 12 states[37]. Anytime a minority group exceeds 26% of the population of the institution, it is very likely the group can exert monopoly power over the rest of the party within the institution. In Mississippi and Georgia, African American populations almost exceed this threshold on their own[38]. In Florida, Hispanics come close to exceeding the threshold, and in Texas they are already far above it[39]. Even when majority control isn't achieved, Asset-based representation delivers equity to minority voters, making it superior to traditional demographic-based systems.

If discrimination is present, the concentration of minorities in one chamber and not the other, greatly improves the influence minority groups have within the individual institutions or the whole legislature. Enhanced representation must be part of any reconstruction effort in order to inoculate

---

[35] Table 1.19 – Southern Reconstruction – Non-owners chamber
[36] Table 1.19 – Southern Reconstruction – Non-owners chamber
[37] Table 1.18 – Southern Reconstruction – Owners chamber
[38] Table 1.18 – Southern Reconstruction – Owners chamber
[39] Table 1.18 – Southern Reconstruction – Owners chamber

the nation from future episodes. When minority groups are discriminated against, it makes it easier for the demographic group to exclude them from the electorate and pass anti-democratic laws that destabilize the nation and make it susceptible to despotism. Asset-based representation makes the country more resilient when minorities have more opportunities to correct discriminatory policies and expand the electorate to all eligible voters.

It is expected that by 2044, non-white populations will have a slight majority over white populations[40]. The significant increase in threats of default and government shutdown within the United States is evidence that the Caucasian populations fear the demographic shift towards plurality and loss in demographic-majority status. The establishment party is terrified over loss of control over the political process, fearing it will result in losses in personal wealth and corporate profits. It is also a fear that former minorities will suddenly reciprocate violence for the generations of economic exploitation and mass incarceration the Caucasian populations used during their reign as demographic-majority group.

Asset-based representation will herald in a period of power sharing before the demographic shift ends, working to avoid any conflict after the nation transitions to plurality. The demographic-majority would have more confidence that the current trajectory in public policy and electoral outcomes would be preserved. Minority groups would have achieved more economic reforms with stronger performance, accepting more modest changes. Most importantly, there would be decades of cooperation and concessions that predated the shift. With less of an expected difference in economic outcomes, the demographic-majority would not resist the demographic shift as much; there should be less corruption, fewer threats of default, less severe shutdowns, and more profits to distribute among the special interest groups.

---

[40] Dudley L. Polston Jr and Rogelio Saenz, "U.S. whites will soon be the minority in number, but not power", Baltimore Sun, Aug 8, 2017, retrieved from https://www.baltimoresun.com/opinion/op-ed/bs-ed-op-0809-minority-majority-20170808-story.html.

In a simulation[41] of the United States based on a macropolitical median partition of homeownership rates, current demographics places 14 states in the lower chamber, 35 states in the upper chamber, and one split between both[42]. The Democrats would have nearly a 55% structural advantage in the lower chamber while the Republicans command a 55% in the upper chamber. Each party will have a significant advantage in one chamber forcing the two to negotiate in good faith. The structural advantages are considerable but not too large to overcome. It is expected that the parties become more competitive within the individual chambers, allowing them to regularly acquire majorities in both chambers.

Political disposition is entirely dependent on the proportion of home ownership in the state which can be altered by public policy. A state could easily pass incentives or regulations that favor home ownership, moving them up in the ranking and possibly changing the chamber location for their representatives. The same is true for demographic changes. When states grow in population, they acquire more representatives while other states lose representatives, altering the rankings and rearranging the composition of the chambers. This reduces the effectiveness of modeling representation based on macropolitical methods, but the uncertainty forces parties to remain more competitive and honest in their practices.

---

[41] For all the simulations provided, the states were allocated to one of the two major parties. This is not intended to be 100% accurate but simply indicative of past or future trends. States allocated to the Democratic side of the ledger are: Vermont, Delaware, Rhode Island, New Hampshire, Maine, New Mexico, Nevada, Hawaii, Connecticut, Wisconsin, Oregon, Minnesota, Maryland, Colorado, Pennsylvania, Washington, Massachusetts, Illinois, New Jersey, New York, California, Michigan. States allocated to the Republican side of the ledger are: North Carolina, South Dakota, Wyoming, North Dakota, Alaska, West Virginia, Montana, Nebraska, Idaho, Arkansas, Iowa, Kansas, Oklahoma, Mississippi, Kentucky, Alabama, Louisiana, Utah, South Carolina, Tennessee, Missouri, Indiana, Arizona, Ohio, Georgia, Virginia, Florida, Texas. The allocations are not arbitrary, but they are subject to changes in demographics and economics. The Democrats could easily lose Michigan, Wisconsin, Colorado or Nevada in any given election while the Republicans could lose Texas, Florida, Virginia, and North Carolina.

[42] Table 1.3 Macropolitical Binary (by State) – Lower Chamber

In a simulation using median home values, there are 23 states in the upper chamber, 26 states in the lower chamber, and one state split between the two chambers. The Republicans control the lower chamber by a margin of 73% to 27% while the Democrats control the upper chamber by a margin of 72% to 28 %[43]. All structural gains in representation earned within one chamber are offset by losses in the other. The two chambers will have to negotiate on every bill in order to pass them through the bicameral process, producing more moderate policies. Unlike the macropolitical partition based on home ownership rate, this system makes it far less likely the parties adopt more moderate policies to make them more competitive in the other chamber; the structural advantage may be too large to overcome with small, nuanced changes in political platform.

The most conventional method for delivering Asset-based representation uses representational coefficients determined by multiplying the median home value by population and then dividing by the total amount by the number of seats in the institution. When using value coefficients, the Democratic states will capture 260 of the 435 seats, roughly equivalent to 60% of the total number of seats[44]. Most of the GDP is located in the Democratic state, resulting in much higher median home values with greater population density[45]. Together, these two properties give the Democratic states a significant institutional advantage over Republican states. Even in off-cycle or midterm elections the residents from the wealthier and more populated states will heavily influence the cadence and substance of the laws passed, forcing the culture of the nation to accommodate the new quality and temper of the laws.

In certain studies, nations with higher GDP tend to preserve their status as democracies for longer than low GDP states[46]. If this tendency is correct, when home values are used

---

[43] Table 1.17 Macropolitical Binary Partition Home Values
[44] Table 1.11 Value Rep Coefficient (all)
[45] Stefan Lembo Stolba, "Median Home Values by State", Experian, Nov 18, 2019, retrieved from https://www.experian.com/blogs/ask-experian/research-/median-home-values-by-state/.
[46] Traditional per capita GDP averages in rural poor regions with urban

as a representational coefficient, all stakeholders can expect better results for the democratization process[47]. If one takes this hypothesis at face value and looks at the per capita GDP adjusted by Asset-based representational coefficients (median home value x population), there is an improvement of 10.7% GDP when examining at the per capita figure for the United States, in terms of GDP per seat[48]. Although modest, a 10.7% improvement in GDP could mean the difference between success and failure in developing nations. If the war efforts can be justified with better results, this will increase the number of attempts and the result is a more secure world.

Adjusted per capita GDP factors in the ratio of proportional representation when determining the measurement of economic activity within a specific region. To calculate the per capita GDP of a specific region, their GDP is multiplied by the number of representatives apportioned to that region. The values from the individual regions are tallied and divided by the total number of representatives, arriving at an adjusted per capita value. An adjusted per capita GDP can then be compared to more traditional per capita GDP calculations when predicting longevity. An increase in per capita GDP demonstrates an increased probability of preserving democracy while a lower figure demonstrates worse outcomes for a newly incorporated nation. The relationship between per capita GDP and longevity changes when the integer value for representation is derivative of econometric variables rather than demographic properties. When the wealthier jurisdictions have more representation, it will change the public policy and electoral outcomes within the nation, and improving the raw propensity for the nation to preserve its status as democracy.

When an adjusted per capita GDP based on median home values and population is used in the United States, the new per capita GDP figure is 10.7% higher than normal per capita GDP figures[49]. An estimate for the current per capita GDP is

---

wealthier neighborhoods which lowers the quality of the analysis.

[47] Those studies that contradicted the claim higher GDP states have extended longevity didn't associate more representation with the higher GDP, so new studies with instrumentalization are needed.

[48] Table 1.12 Value Per Capita Rep (all)

$54,344 with an adjusted per capita GDP coming in at $60,158 for an improvement of more than $5,814[50]. If adjusted per capita GDP has similar effects on other states, the 10.7% increase in per capita GDP may be enough to influence the longevity of newly incorporated democratic nations[51]. More telling is the breakdown in per capita GDP when the Democratic states are separated from the Republican states. When the new per capita GDP of $59,118 for the Democratic states is compared to the former U.S. per capita GDP of $54,344.00, it demonstrates a net change of $4,774 for 8.78% improvement in per capita GDP[52]. When the adjusted per capita GDP of $66,154 for Democratic states is compared to the new per capita GDP figure of $59,118, it produces a net change of $7,036 for a 11.90% improvement in representation[53].

Republican states net a loss of $3,752 for a 6.90% reduction in per capita GDP when the former per capita GDP of $54,344 for the combined United States is compared to the new per capita GDP of $50,592[54]. After an adjusted per capita GDP of $51,211 for Republican states is compared to the traditional per capita GDP of $50,592, it produces a meager $619 improvement in representation, or 1.22%[55] Most of the benefits for adjusted per capita GDP favor the Democratic states when they are split from the Republican states. If the new per capita GDP of $59,118 for Democratic states is compared to the new per capita GDP for Republican states of $50,592, it demonstrates an $8,526 (or 16.85%) advantage for the Democratic states over the Republican States. The advantage is even more pronounced when adjusted per capita GDP is compared between the Democratic states and Republican States; the Democratic states have an adjusted per capita GDP of $66,154 compared to the adjusted per capita

---

49 Table 1.12 Value Per Capita Rep (all)
50 Table 1.12 Value Per Capita Rep (all)
51 Adam Przeworski, Minimalist Conception of Democracy: A Defense." In Democracy's Value edited by Shapiro, I. and Hacker-Cordon, C. (Cambridge: Cambridge University), page 16.
52 Table 1.10 Value Per Capita Rep (Democratic)
53 Table 1.10 Value Per Capita Rep (Democratic)
54 Table 1.8 Value Per Capita Representation (Republican)
55 Table 1.8 Value Per Capita Representation (Republican)

GDP of $51,211 for Republican states, resulting in a $14,943 (or 29.18%) advantage for Democratic states.

The effect of higher GDP may be less in more industrialized nations like the United States, but this highlights the dramatic effect adjusted per capita GDP may have in other scenarios. Less industrialized nations may have lower per capita GDP and adjusted per capita GDPs, but the proportion of change could be higher indicating an effect with greater magnitude change in longevity. This type of analysis is also useful in real time, during secession movements or other sources of instability. Looking at per capita GDP figures will help allies predict the viability of relationships, in expectation of performance after conflict. At the very least, alternative systems of democracy provide multiple possible outcomes, where new governments can attract stakeholders and investors to improve their performance during and after an event

4 PROTEST MOVEMENTS

Peaceful protests are the most effective strategy for pursuing political reform. "Nonviolent protests are twice as likely to succeed as armed conflicts – and those engaging a threshold of 3.5% of the population have never failed to bring about change"[56]. This 3.5% threshold is not easy to meet and authoritarian parties will do everything in their power to disrupt the protests and inhibit support for the social movement, but when this threshold is exceeded, it almost always results in reform or regime change. It has yet to be tested, but institutional protests, like government shutdowns, may act as a force multiplier when protests acquire only 1-3% of the population, allowing much smaller movements to acquire the same degree of success larger movements earn when they exceed the 3.5% threshold.

When seeking concessions and reforms, general strikes "are probably one of the most powerful, if not the most powerful, single method of nonviolent resistance"[57]. Government shutdowns are equivalent to general strikes in that they shut down the appropriations power of the government, immediately pausing non-essential agencies

---

[56] David Robson, "The '3.5% rule': How a small minority can change the world", BBC, May 13, 2019, retrieved from https://www.bbc.com/future-/article/20190513-it-only-takes-35-of-people-to-change-the-world.
[57] David Robson, "The '3.5% rule': How a small minority can change the world", BBC, May 13, 2019, retrieved from https://www.bbc.com/future-/article/20190513-it-only-takes-35-of-people-to-change-the-world.

within the discretionary portion of the budget. They are a statement on the commitment to peaceful resistance to a regime for quick reconciliation and compromise. More importantly, it forces an admission that democracies require the consent of the governed.

All evidence suggests that peaceful protest is far more effective than violence at achieving reforms. "Overall, nonviolent campaigns were twice as likely to succeed as violent campaigns: they led to political change 53% of the time compared to 26% for the violent protests"[58]. One reason for this large difference in success rates may be participation. "Overall, the nonviolent campaigns attracted around four times as many participants (200,000) as the average violent campaign (50,000)"[59]. Institutional protests, like government shutdowns, should increase participation rates even further, adding credibility to the movement, and limiting the government's ability to disrupt them with interventions by the police and military.

The presence of institutional protests will give the protest movement enough time to mobilize the 3.5% of the public needed to acquire reform. In oppressive regimes, an authoritarian parties' quick and violent response may quash support for the movement before it gains the critical mass needed for reform. When the government is denied emergency funding, it will not be able to deploy the police assets or military needed to put down the uprising. When political parties support the protest movement with institutional protests, it gives permission to a much larger audience to become engaged in the debate and performance. The heightened attention will focus the public on arguments supporting peaceful protest, while signaling to the establishment party that there will be electoral consequences if violence is used. A larger turnout at the protest almost

---

[58] David Robson, "The '3.5% rule': How a small minority can change the world", BBC, May 13, 2019, retrieved from https://www.bbc.com/future-/article/20190513-it-only-takes-35-of-people-to-change-the-world.
[59] David Robson, "The '3.5% rule': How a small minority can change the world", BBC, May 13, 2019, retrieved from https://www.bbc.com/future-/article/20190513-it-only-takes-35-of-people-to-change-the-world.

guarantees more voters at the polling stations, even if elections are several months or years later.

Government shutdowns and peaceful protests complement each other in intent and effect. "Chenoweth argues that nonviolent campaigns are generally easier to discuss openly, which means that news of their occurrence can reach a wider audience. Violent movements, on the other hand, require a supply of weapons, and tend to rely on more secretive underground operations that might struggle to reach the general population"[60]. Institutional protests split the difference. They are harder to organize than protests, but a shutdown can make both peaceful protests and violent movements much more effective. If the government uses violence against a peaceful protest movement supported by an institutional protest, the movement can quickly transition into an armed rebellion after the institutional protest shuts down the appropriations process, curtails tax revenues, or destroys the credit of the nation.

All government shutdowns complement protests movements with the expectation their support will increase the participation above the 3.5% threshold. More of the public will be willing to take to the streets when politicians back their verbal support with policy. A government shutdown is more than evidence of support, it is imminent aid. The federal government is put on a clock, where current funds will run out, with no capacity to borrow or appropriate additional funds until concessions are made. This is an ultimatum; accept reform or break the government. The authoritarians may still decide to prosecute a war because they are facing poor election outcomes or prosecution, but if they do, they will do so in an inferior position, without appropriations and borrowing authority, when a large number of states have organized a resistance to them.

Unlike violent insurrection, which is permanent and irreversible in harm done to individuals and states, institutional protests can be mitigated or compensated after implementation. Much of the economic harm by institutional

---

[60] David Robson, "The '3.5% rule': How a small minority can change the world", BBC, May 13, 2019, retrieved from https://www.bbc.com/future-/article/20190513-it-only-takes-35-of-people-to-change-the-world.

protests can be reversed with cash subsidies, tax breaks, and reparations. There is another advantage. Institutional protests have severe economic consequences, but they can't be compared to the death and disability that accompany armed insurrection. Institutional protests occur in slow motion, over the course of weeks and months, in the spotlight of the public, where all concerned residents, citizens, and elected officials have an opportunity to form opinions and price those into future elections or public policy.

The threat of institutional protests should elevate the success rate above 53%, once authoritarian regimes understand the implied risk institutional protests pose to establishment governments. Authoritarian parties cloak themselves in the belief that their superior position grants them access to policing power and military power that could put down any rebellion. Debt defaults, tax protests, and prolonged government shutdowns eliminate the advantages of occupying the federal executive office, and once the illusion of power is dispelled by the realities of institutional protests, the authoritarian parties may be more open to compromises and concessions towards democracy.

Peaceful protests work in 53% of situations, but this strategy still fails nearly 47% of the time. When authoritarianism is threatening the nation, leaving it up to chance is not appropriate. Institutional Protests optimize the protest movement's position in case the peaceful protests fail, and the only recourse is state-organized rebellion. States retain the authority to act where individuals don't. States are political organisms made up of thousands or millions of persons, including both residents and citizens, giving them a much more accurate perspective to base their decisions on. As the number of voters increase, the state can arrive at more accurate conclusions on complex issues. They see more perspectives and can reach compromises with larger portions of the population. When more of the public is satisfied with public policy, there is more trust and less dissent. If the policies fail, voters will support other candidates and parties, allowing the state to correct their priorities. When an individual acts, they act in their own interests, but when the state acts, it acts within the communities' interests.

The aggregation of interests allows states to take acts that would otherwise be illegal for individuals. However, this is far from a perfect rationalization. A democratic state's actions may be supported by 55% of the public, but this also means 45% of the public objects to the behavior. Unilateral actions by the state disregard the preferences of a large portion of the electorate. And although, the states retain their authority, it certainly introduces a measurement of how legitimate specific actions are. If one looks at it in terms of partial authority rather than unilateral or ultimate authority, the state may have the right to act, but it can be questioned by its residents, citizens, and more importantly, other states or governments. The political parties must respect future outcomes from elections, forcing them to take the opposition parties' positions into consideration. With this in mind, states are much better off supporting non-violent and peaceful strategies, like institutional protests, rather than armed rebellions.

Oftentimes violence can't be avoided but it is not always up to the protest movement. No matter how disciplined and patient the protesters are, they are not the only parties involved in the conflict. There is a significant possibility an authoritarian government responds to peaceful movements with violence, where the police provoke riots and mobs instead of promoting order. Hardened authoritarians will predictably rely on violence and mass incarceration to rein in protest movements and curtail opposition parties. Every encounter has the potential for violence and disaster, which is why the risk scales up with the participation rate of the public. When 3.5% of the public is engaged with the protest movement, it presents a large number of opportunities for police sponsored violence or rioting, increasing the systemic risk to the state by way of regime change or violence.

The overwhelming majority of force used during protests are by the police, corporations, or federal authorities, skewing the statistics for violent protests. The violence used by the establishment is usually excused, validated by their position, rather than moral standards. Protesters often retaliate with violence when provoked by overly oppressive police forces but the incidents are recorded as inexcusable criminal acts. Peaceful protests are more effective because they give zero opportunity for the media or authorities to discredit them. When most of the demonstrations and strikes remain peaceful, the movement has a greater chance of acquiring critical mass and achieving the reforms sought.

If peaceful movements remain disciplined and are still brutalized by the police, it demonstrates to the larger population that peaceful nonresistance is not effective, and the numbers of violent participants will grow to previously unexpressed levels. Peaceful protests have four times as much participation as violent protests, but the ratio will change after the lawful protests are violently suppressed. It will be understood throughout the entire population that there is only one way to force regime change or reform, and that is through violence. A larger portion of the public will start to organize themselves and mobilize for active resistance or war. Their elected leaders can support them with a government shutdown, followed by tax protests, and finally debt defaults, optimizing their chances of reasserting their civil rights.

Institutional protests are much more effective at neutralizing a government's ability to deploy law enforcement or military assets in order to prevent an insurrection, while also raising awareness and support for the movement in the public's eye. If the authoritarian regime attempts to disregard the preference of 3.5% of the public, and use the police or military to suppress them, their actions will quickly take on criminal properties when prohibited by the legislature with embargos on appropriations. Authoritarians rely on the legitimacy of their policing power and if they are acting in direct contradiction of the constitution or congress, a much larger portion of the public will defect to the protesters side. This opens the door for impeachment and removal from office. Nothing is guaranteed but shutting down the government creates more possibilities for regime change and reform, than peaceful protests do alone.

When peaceful negotiations fail, opposition parties will want to exercise every advantage they have access to improve the 26% success rate. Disrupting government services and diverting their revenues is one of the more effective strategies rebel groups can pursue. It is estimated that combat only comprises about 5% of the effort during rebellions, community cohesion results in 80% of the work, and disrupting government services results in approximately 15% of the struggle[61]. When the rebel states become the sole provider of security and government services, they can more aggressively pursue regime change in other regions and other revolutionary policies. Many of the more successful insurgencies in the 20th century has followed this model[62].

Institutional protests are the newest and best strategy insurgents can employ to completely disrupt the current regime's ability to provide government services and security. When the federal government's debts are defaulted on, their revenues diverted to state governments, and all budget appropriation ended, it will be the local and state governments that assume the role of service provider and guarantor of security. Rebel groups can immediately step in with their own government services after disrupting the finances and services of the federal government. Most taxes are collected by firms domiciled within the states allowing rebel governments to easily divert the tax revenues away from the federal government by targeting businesses and their owners. When the states assume the former federal tax revenues, they can quickly onboard federal enlisted and personnel defecting due to compromised pay.

When opposition parties pursue institutional protests, it can't be construed as sedition. Sedition is an overt attempt to overthrow the government, but in democracies the process is more important than the principals. The president can't be confused with the state and the state can't be confused with the president. Sedition requires planning for overt physical violence against the government while institutional protests rely on lawful due process and nonviolence to coerce regime change. Using a government shutdown to remove a president is not an attempt to overthrow democracy if the constitution remains intact and unviolated. The principals may change but the system of government remains the same.

When opposition parties pursue regime change, the administration refusing to abdicate implicitly accepts the terms

---

[61] William Polk, "Violent Politics",(New York: harper Collins, 2007), pp. xvi.
[62] William Polk, "Violent Politics",(New York: harper Collins, 2007), pp. xvi.

of the lawful shutdown. It is an impasse with the current president remaining in office while the federal government is denied all appropriations and borrowing authority. Both parties are making the decision that a defunded federal government is the optimal outcome for the present circumstances. The nation may remain shut down until the next election cycle, even if that is several years later. If the opposition party is resolute, the federal government can be shut down for the entire term of the illegitimate president. It is risky but the threat of an authoritarian consolidating power and corrupting future elections is more dangerous.

The legality of institutional protests is evidenced by their ubiquitous use in the United States. Institutional protests increased in frequency from just 2 incidents in the first 200 years to 20 incidents in the last 50 years. There were only two near defaults in the United States history prior to the Civil Rights Movement. One default occurred in 1933 during the Great Depression and the other near default occurred in the 1870s after the American Civil War[63]. Since 1965, there have been 20 separate events, ranging from government shutdowns lasting just 1 day to shutdowns lasting a few weeks[64]. The frequency of these threats has increased by nearly 50 times. They have become more severe too, growing in length from an average of 3 days to nearly 30 days, with the most recent shutdown persisting for more than 8% of the entire year[65].

The filibuster is another form of institutional protest and it has seen an equivalent increase frequency and severity. The filibuster was a rule created 30 years after the Constitution was ratified and should not be confused with any amendment or delegated power. During from 1919 until 1969, it was only used 49 times and was easily overcome with a second round of voting[66]. On average, a filibustered bill passed an average of

---

[63] Infoplease Staff, "Timeline of U.S. Government Shutdowns", Infoplease, updated March 17, 2020, retrieved from https://www.infoplease.com/history/-us/timeline-of-us-government-shutdowns.

[64] Infoplease Staff, "Timeline of U.S. Government Shutdowns", Infoplease, updated March 17, 2020, retrieved from https://www.infoplease.com/history/-us/timeline-of-us-government-shutdowns.

[65] Infoplease Staff, "Timeline of U.S. Government Shutdowns", Infoplease, updated March 17, 2020, retrieved from https://www.infoplease.com/history/-us/timeline-of-us-government-shutdowns

13 days later, which is much different than the contemporary use. In the last 50 years, there has been nearly 1,073 filibusters resulting in a 2100% increase in the number measures[67]. These days, once a bill is filibustered, it remains filibustered until it can overcome a 60 Senator margin. Worse, "Cloture is now a de facto requirement for the passage of any significant measure", meaning the filibuster impacts all laws debated, effectively raising the numbers of senators needed to pass any law to 60% rather than 51%[68]. This is unprecedented in the history of democracies, which typically only require a simple majority to pass laws.

If institutional protests were not inherently lawful and based on due process, the political parties would not have had enough confidence to use them as much as they have in the last 50 years. The first time a party shutdown the government, the leaders of the opposition party would be sent to prison for decades long sentences. The first time a party willfully threatened debt defaults in order to coerce reforms would be the last as the party members would be removed from office and incarcerated. They have not been threatened with sedition because it is a lawful exercise and fully supported by due process and the U.S. Constitution. If a party wants to end a government shutdown, they will have to meet the demand of the opposition party, or be willing to wait it out until the next election cycle when those legislators can be voted out of office.

Using peaceful and nonviolent protests to enact social and political change is the gold standard for participation in the democratic process, but is not a means in its own. Peaceful protest must be supported by political parties willing to use force to protect the protesters. State governments can offer protesters some protections but most movements need the

---

[66] Josh Chavetz, "The Unconstitutionality or the Filibuster".
Connecticut Law Review, pp. 1009, May 201, retrieved from https://papers.-ssrn.com/sol3/-papers.-cfm?abstract_id=1730782
[67] Josh Chavetz "The Unconstitutionality or the Filibuster".
Connecticut Law Review, pp. 1009, May 201, retrieved from https://papers.-ssrn.com/sol3/-papers.-cfm?abstract_id=1730782
[68] Josh Chavetz, "The Unconstitutionality or the Filibuster".
Connecticut Law Review, pp. 1008, May 201, retrieved from https://papers.-ssrn.com/sol3/-papers.-cfm?abstract_id=1730782

support of a federal government or a coalition of democratic governments. Despotic regimes fearing reprisal from democracies, and state governments that fear oversight from federal institutions, will hesitate, and within this short window of opportunity a movement can gain the critical mass needed for reform and regime change. If there is no oversight or expectations of reprisals, the local despot can act us aggressively to subdue the resistance movement, ruthlessly oppressing the people before more gain the courage to mobilize and demand reform.

When opposition parties threaten government shutdowns and debt defaults, the authoritarian government is denied borrowing authority and appropriations authority and it can't act to disrupt or discourage the peaceful protests. The movement will gain momentum and popularity, helping facilitate a peaceful regime change or pass reforms to cure the leadership of its authoritarian defects. If there is no implied force, authoritarians won't respect the civil liberties and voting rights of their citizens. When an administration maintains its authority to borrow money and appropriate it to law enforcement or military agencies, it can use these assets to put down peaceful movements with no recourse for protesters and no consequences for officials. The threat of force is the ultimate determinant of whether a protest movement is successful; this force can be violent, as in police batons and tear gas, or peaceful when a political party imposes a government shutdown.

Without the recourse of legislative force or martial force, there is only a perception or illusion of peace. Any state can be preserved indefinitely if the minority party accepts the deteriorating conditions in exchange for personal guarantees of safety. Appeasement and collaboration are the twin evils of civil society. Those in positions of privilege can keep their wealth and power as long as they don't challenge the current regime. The fear of loss will be so great, that anybody in a position to resist, won't because those earning the disfavor of the authoritarian government are usually incarcerated or murdered.

If political parties do not support their protesting constituents with institutional protest, they may not acquire meaningful protest numbers, and they miss their only opportunity to resolve the electoral issues with peaceful means. Worse, if the opposition party does not use institutional protests to improve their chances of winning a conflict, they risk being overwhelmed by a fully funded federal government. There will be no defections, the establishment government won't have any issues borrowing, and enlisted will dutifully follow the orders of the military hierarchy. The opposition party will likely only have a small window of opportunity to protest a compromised election, before the precedent is set for further interventions, and future elections can't be trusted.

The probability of successfully defending democracy is directly proportional to the courage the opposition party has to organize an immediate response. If the opposition party doesn't think they can successfully defend the nation or their states, they will cooperate with the authoritarian party. If the nation already has low quality democratic entitlements, influenced by deregulated campaign finance, voter ID laws, voter registration purges, computerized gerrymandering, and other deleterious public policies, the opposition party can disguise their collaboration in negligence and ignorance. This is the worst-case scenario, where there is no resistance to the decline into authoritarianism.

Democratic parties must fear the arrow of time; after one bad election cycle, they could permanently lose access to the majorities needed for an institutional protest such as a government shutdown or debt default. If they can't resist authoritarianism from within the government, they will have to organize resistance to it on the outside. Democrats must carefully weigh the odds of success, versus the probability of incarceration, disability, death. It is an unfair burden, which is why so many democratic parties choose to collaborate, and democracies fall into despotism.

The pain of losing democracy will only be temporary as those citizens that joined organized resistance will be incarcerated or murdered, leaving alive and free only those who supported the totalitarian regime. Within a single generation, respect for non-democratic institutions can be taught through violence and illiberal incentives. The public will focus on protecting their immediate families, and cease taking risks for neighbors, coworkers, or others. They will sit idle as the government weans the most vulnerable and aspirational from the ranks of the youth. This is how the culture of despotism roots in a nation that previously held ideals on discourse and due process.

5 THREATS OF DEFAULT

Institutional protests are a new form of asymmetric warfare that present the best opportunity for opposition parties to win wars of succession or secession in democratic nations. When a military power has a tenfold advantage in resources, they win 71.5% of all conventional military engagements[69]. However, the odds of a conventional military power winning drops to just 36.4% when these rebel groups use unconventional tactics like guerrilla warfare[70]. If rebel groups refuse to fight conventional wars, they win 63.6% of the time. Institutional protests, such as debt defaults and prolonged government shutdowns, are forms of asymmetric warfare that will change the odds in favor of a rebel group or opposition party. All democracies live with constraints placed on them by the treasury; when a lack of appropriation powers choke off revenues and borrowing become impossible, establishment governments will be forced to negotiate concessions or risk losing the war.

Even when facing overwhelming odds, smaller and less organized rebel forces still have a 28.5% chance of winning. All military conflicts carry a significant risk of loss, which produces an incentive towards concessions and negotiated

---

[69] Ivan Arreguin-Toft, "How the Weak Win Wars: A Theory of Asymmetric Conflict", International Security, Vol. 26, No. 1 (Summer 2001), pp. 93–128.
[70] Ivan Arreguin-Toft, "How the Weak Win Wars: A Theory of Asymmetric Conflict", International Security, Vol. 26, No. 1 (Summer 2001), pp. 93–128.

peace. Prolonged government shutdowns and threats of default are such powerful inducements to peaceful regime change or reform, that the opposition party is more likely to avoid violent conflict by explicitly describing the consequences and risks beforehand. When establishment governments face a precipitous drop in winning percentages, falling from 71.5% to just 36.4%, where loss carries risk of death or incarceration for government officials, declaring an intent to shut down the government or default should be enough to coerce the administration into agreeing to a concession ending the standoff. Discouraging the establishment party from using violence to put down protestors, gives the opposition party an opportunity to pass reforms and win subsequent elections, effectively diffusing the situation.

If the current administration can't be persuaded to leave office or commit to reforms, the opposition party is in an optimal position to escalate the conflict. Before even taking up arms against an authoritarian, rebels can destroy the government's ability to borrow with a debt default and lock down all new appropriations with a government shutdown. Armies run on money and without deficit financing, a substantial portion of the armed forces can't be deployed. All new enlistments and new arms purchase require additional funding with separate appropriations. They will be prevented by the shutdown, forcing the establishment party to rely on state-level appropriations, law enforcement, and state militia deployments, thus, elevating the rebel movement to near equal standing with the federal military,

Most establishment governments will resist deferring to lower level governments for an organized response to the rebel threat, causing a severe delay in the intensity and speed of a response. When an establishment government hesitates, the probability of successfully defending the nation drops to just 36.4%. The establishment party has to be careful that their stalled response doesn't result in a complete loss and occupation of allied states. Secession is the more immediate threat, but if protest groups successfully destabilize the federal government, and its allied states don't prepare a response, they can be defeated by conventional means, resulting in occupation.

The most certain way to create a permanent advantage for rebels is to default on the nation's debt. It is a single standalone act that will have long lasting consequences for an establishment government. Not only will new borrowing be at a significantly higher rate, but any roll-over debt will also be affected. To put this in perspective, the United States currently pays 8.7% of all government outlays to interest on more than $22T in debt[71]. These outlays include Social Security and Medicare so if one looks at the discretionary parts of the budget, current deficit financing is closer to 14% of government outlays. Interest rates on Treasury debt are at an all-time low now, but if the U.S. were to default, it could more than double or triple debt servicing costs for the federal government.

If the debt was defaulted on, and interest rates doubled, the net interest portion of the budget could rise to 28% of the discretionary budget. The standing army would be denied valuable financial resources, endangering their ability to equip and deploy soldiers during an emergency. Current defense appropriations only account for current expenditures, and not those costs associated with responding to an armed insurrection or secessionist movement. A prolonged government shutdown will likely follow, eliminating the possibility of securing additional appropriations despite urgent need for new expenditures to respond to the insurgency.

Once a default occurs, it may be impossible to resurrect the federal government. If the nation normally pays 14% of its revenues in debt liabilities, a default immediately requires spending cuts of at least 14% when the interest rate owed on the obligations double. If the country operated with a 3% deficit and borrowing becomes impossible, another 20% in cuts would be needed to compensate for the unsupported spending. In total, the administration would need to implement cuts in excess of 34% just to keep even.

The government's discretionary spending would be severely compromised, with more than half of all revenues going to debt servicing and the rest to the military, making it

---

[71] Drew Desilver, "5 facts about the national debt", Pew Research Center, July 24, 2019, retrieved from https://www.pewresearch.org/fact-tank/2019/07/24/facts-about-the-national-debt/.

impossible to deliver healthcare, manage prisons, industrial regulations, provide law enforcement, and tax collection. The people would cease to trust the government and view it as an asset. On paper, the federal government would be worth more if all of its properties were sold off and the federal debt discharged. Large portions of the population would call for it to be dissolved, fearing the nation may never recover.

If the opposition parties' legislators act on their threats to default, the only strategy the establishment party has left it to declare the acts as treason and arresting them. This strategy is full of risks when the authority to cause a default is explicit. From the onset, the establishment party will be mired in legal proceedings with uncertain outcomes. Arresting the opposition party and failing to convict them, may embolden their constituents in the next election cycle. Worse, failing to convict the legislators might legitimize the act and promote even more radical behaviors. Even if the legislators are removed from office, it won't likely result in the majorities the establishment party needs to avoid other institutional protests. In the United States, governors are allowed to appoint legislators to open seats until a special election is held. The political party organizing the rebellion will be able to appoint other radicals or supporters of secession in the place of those that were arrested for treason.

Debt defaults are extraordinary measures which should only be considered when the democratic process is threatened. The effects are immediate with consequences so deleterious that is could take decades for a nation to recover from the default. Businesses and individuals would stop making new purchases[72]. Companies will furlough and lay off workers and unemployment would increase significantly. A default would hurt the value of the dollar, price increase for food and other commodities. interest rates would go up for business, individuals and the government[73]. This could herald in

---

[72] Jeff Cox, "What's the worst that could happen? 7 debt-default doomsday scenarios", NBC News, Oct 10, 2013, retrieved from
https://www.nbcnews.com/businessmain/whats-worst-could-happen-7-debt-default-doomsday-scenarios-8C11366851.
[73] Jeff Cox, "What's the worst that could happen? 7 debt-default doomsday scenarios", NBC News, Oct 10, 2013, retrieved from

consumer debt defaults, mortgage defaults, foreclosures, and business defaults. Investments in 401k, pension, and other funds would go down or negative[74]. The lack of performance will restrict revenues for companies who relied on stock sales or who borrowed against their value. With fewer people working governments would have less sales, payroll, and income taxes.

Investors will see portfolios shift when the value of government debt drop precipitously, impacting the borrowing capacity of nations like China and Japan who buy large amounts of government debt. Many financial firms and banks also buy and sell government debt, raising rates all over the word, causing defaults in developing nations and strained economies everywhere. There would be certainly capital flight out of the country that defaulted[75]. Investors would take their money out of the economies fearing more political instability or economic blowback. The government would have to stop paying salaries for soldiers and officials[76]. National pensions and healthcare payments would immediately stop too[77].

Essential services, which typically stay open during a government shutdown, would immediately cease[78]. In most government shutdowns there is a secondary agreement that keeps the payments going, but a prolonged shutdown will invariably lead to the end of any agreement on appropriations for both essential and non-essential services. Although

---

https://www.nbcnews.com/businessmain/whats-worst-could-happen-7-debt-default-doomsday-scenarios-8C11366851.

[74] Jeff Cox, "What's the worst that could happen? 7 debt-default doomsday scenarios", NBC News, Oct 10, 2013, retrieved from https://www.nbcnews.com/businessmain/whats-worst-could-happen-7-debt-default-doomsday-scenarios-8C11366851.

[75] Scotty Hendricks, "What would happen if America defaulted on its debt?", Big Think, Nov 15, 2018, retrieved from https://bigthink.com/politics-current-affairs/what-if-the-government-defaults.

[76] Scotty Hendricks, "What would happen if America defaulted on its debt?", Big Think, Nov 15, 2018, retrieved from https://bigthink.com/politics-current-affairs/what-if-the-government-defaults.

[77] Scotty Hendricks, "What would happen if America defaulted on its debt?", Big Think, Nov 15, 2018, retrieved from https://bigthink.com/politics-current-affairs/what-if-the-government-defaults.

[78] Scotty Hendricks, "What would happen if America defaulted on its debt?", Big Think, Nov 15, 2018, retrieved from https://bigthink.com/politics-current-affairs/what-if-the-government-defaults.

military budgets may be protected from short-term shutdowns with mandatory funding, most of those outlays are for peace-time expenditures. Protesting states can organize and mobilize without much fear of federal intervention if they maintain the government shutdown and don't authorize any new appropriations. Despite peace-time budgets already being approved, no extra-ordinary expenditures are covered. Even if a federal government is able to finesse a response with short-term reserves, the funding will eventually be exhausted, and all authority to prosecute the war will end.

Debt defaults are permanent and irrevocable making them an institutional protest of last resort. One of the only times a debt default is warranted is when the quality of elections is compromised past the point of redemption, and the only cure for the failures in leadership is the destruction of the illiberal or authoritarian government. A government that is no longer responsive to the people through democratic elections must be defunded and disabled before it can consolidate its new unaccountable power with loyalist law enforcement and the threat of military intervention. The opposition party will have to strike with resolve, discipline, and lightning speed or they may find recourse by debt default out of reach.

If the legitimacy of a debt default depends on the quality of elections, political parties will be able to arbitrarily call election outcomes invalid and set up a plausible threat of default, despite any evidence supporting those conclusions. Political parties often rely on discretion and personal preferences instead of facts, resulting in supporters who are extremely tolerant of lies and misdirection. In a miasma of untruth, political parties can advocate for debt defaults, not because they are legitimate responses to corruption, but because they provide better outcomes than accepting electoral losses.

The biggest risk of a debt default occurs when a party expects to win office but loses in a close election. For example, if the Republican candidate wins the 2020 election, it will result in the Republican party winning nearly 64% of all presidential elections since President Nixon[79]. If the

---

[79] Editors of Encyclopedia Britannica, "United States Presidential Election

Republicans were to lose, they would compare the 64% likelihood to the 0% realized outcome and come to the conclusion the election was stolen or compromised in some manner, justifying threats to permanently disfigure the country with a debt default. The psychological operation is even more pronounced during a demographic shift, where there is a fear of never winning again, throwing a lot of zeros into the average expected outcomes they are basing their judgement on.

If a Democrat wins and remains in office for 8 years, the Republican winning percentage drops to just over 53% from 62%[80]. A 9% reduction in winning percentage equals a loss of nearly 15% in competitiveness. When the Republican winning percentage drops to just 53%, it signals the best outcomes are only as good as a coin toss. If they don't change their belief systems, the probability of winning will drop even more, retroactively confirming their suspicions about being relegated to a minority position. It is also unlikely the Republicans will accept the same lackluster 39% winning percentage the Democrats persisted under for the last 50 odd years. They will confuse the historic electoral outcomes from an all-white and mostly male electorate over the last 250 years, with their performance over the last few decades, and over-react when their win percentage drops to more rational expectations.

The threats of default exhibit the lack of inhibitions and a sense of urgency that is only there if predicated on a race-based expectation of losing majority political power. Competitive political parties should only win 50% of the elections. An ebbing demographic-majority should be equally distributed among both parties, with an equal probability of winning election. This is not evident in a 2012 survey of the United States, where Republicans are composed of 89% non-Hispanic white voters and the Democrats just 60%[81]. The

---

Results", Encyclopedia Britannica, accessed on July 17, 2020, Retrieved from https://www.britannica.com/topic/United-States-Presidential-Election-Results-1788863.

[80] Editors of Encyclopedia Britannica, "United States Presidential Election Results", Encyclopedia Britannica, accessed on July 17, 2020, Retrieved from https://www.britannica.com/topic/United-States-Presidential-Election-Results-1788863.

[81] Frank Newport, "Democrats Racially Diverse; Republicans Mostly White",

proportion of Non-Hispanic African Americans in the Republican party is just 2% compared to 22% in the Democratic party[82]. Only 6% of the Republican party is Hispanic versus 13% of the Democratic Party[83]. This lopsided participation is due to wealth inequality and discrimination, perpetuating a demographic-based winner take all system.

The severe drop in winning percentage doesn't only represent an immediate loss of political power, it represents a future where Caucasians are in a minority with little opportunity to defend their wealth and property. There is a long history of abuse and exploitation in the United States, including the genocide of Native Americans, enslavement of African Americans, and the exclusion of women and poor white males from the electorate. The Caucasian populations fear being treated as badly as they have treated others, in a system designed to exploit and oppress minorities. Fear of retaliatory violence will provoke them into doubting the integrity of elections with complete mistrust of government. When parties are confident, they can win re-election, they will simply pass budgets of their choice and laws in their favor. If the party loses confidence in their ability to win elections, they will lose confidence in the nation, and start to resent it as an illegitimate authority. This appears to be the arc of the United States and its GOP; a growing portion of the Republican constituencies will support secession when they realize they won't continue winning 62% of the Presidential elections.

Gallup, Feb 8, 2013, retrieved from https://news.gallup.com/poll/160373-/democrats-racially-diverse-republicans-mostly-white.aspx.

[82] Frank Newport, "Democrats Racially Diverse; Republicans Mostly White", Gallup, Feb 8, 2013, retrieved from https://news.gallup.com/poll/160373/-democrats-racially-diverse-republicans-mostly-white.aspx.

[83] Frank Newport, "Democrats Racially Diverse; Republicans Mostly White", Gallup, Feb 8, 2013, retrieved from https://news.gallup.com/poll/-160373/democrats-racially-diverse-republicans-mostly-white.aspx.

6 TAX PROTESTS

The party that practices more will have faster recall and better production during a crisis. If one party prefers ideologies focused on state rights, they are more likely to respond to government shutdowns with state-level executive orders and prepared public policies. If they regularly rehearse with threats of government shutdowns and debt defaults, they will have more discipline to deploy them when actually needed. Political parties that inculcate their constituents in the rhetoric of institutional protests can depend on more support from an engaged public when they do respond to a threat. All in all, the better practiced party should be favored in a conflict with a party relies on bipartisanship federal actions to resolve issues while in office.

Those parties depending on the federal government to legislate or act during crises will be caught by surprise when the federal government is shut down or its finances ruined with a default. Political parties may mistakenly believe that the next election cycle will end the threat. They will over-emphasize waiting until the results of the election are known. Not only might they party lose the election, but the other party might not respect the outcome, resisting a peaceful transfer of power. If the establishment party waits too long, they may miss their opportunity to intervene and defend the nation against a secession or fascist overthrow of the democracy. The longer they wait, the more likely a dissolution or occupation results from the conflict.

There are limits to the effectiveness of institutional protests84. A government shutdown doesn't affect exempted parts of the budget or multi-year funding authorizations, allowing the police and military to continue operations. However, even exempted agencies can't take on new spending and obligations85. These agencies and departments cannot make the extra expenditures needed to support a war effort or counter-protest movement. Within a short few weeks or months, they will run out of their current funding and require supplemental appropriations. If the government shutdown remains in place, this funding will be denied, immediately ending the operations. If this budgetary check was not in place, an imperial president or authoritarian could simply dissolve the legislature and maintain its own funding of war time activities to suppress democratic resistance.

Although excepted agencies can continue to operate, they may not pay their employees until a new funding deal is reached. This is the crux of the institutional protest. If there is no intent on passing a new budget, there is no expectation of passing new appropriations for national security, military, and law enforcement agency employees. Without the expectation of future payment, even the excepted agencies must shut down. Legally, excepted workers can only work with the expectation of a future budget being passed. If this is a prolonged government shutdown, lasting over 6 months and up to 2 years, there is no expectation of resolution. In practice, many of the enlisted and law enforcement will have to resign after not receiving pay, to seek work on the state level or private sector. The longer the government shutdown lasts, the more effective it is in denying the establishment party the advantages inherent to a federal government.

One of the biggest risks to a shutdown is if the government arrests federal legislators for participating in the

---

[84] U.S. Office of Personnel Management, "Guidance for Shutdown Furloughs", Sept 2015, Office of Personnel Management, retrieved from https://www.opm.gov/policy-data-oversight/pay-leave/furlough-guidance/guidance-for-shutdown-furloughs.pdf.
[85] Congressional Research Service, "Shutdown of the Federal Government: Causes, Processes, and Effects", Congressional Research Service, RL34680, Updated Dec 10, 2018, retrieved from https://fas.org/sgp/crs/misc/-RL34680.pdf.

protest. Many legislators may resist participating in a government shutdown out of fear of reprisals. This is not true for governors, who can protect themselves with state police and the national guard if threatened with illicit incarceration. More importantly, governors can augment their militias with state and local police, supporting them with locally sourced food, housing, and munitions. During longer protests, governors can completely obstruct the supply chains and revenues crippling federal military and law enforcement is used to put down the rebellious states. All of these actions are available without the implicit support by federal legislators pursing a government shutdown or default.

Tax protests are the most effective strategy for protest when the establishment government disregards the constitution and continues authorizing expenditures. Tax protests are the only institutional protest that do not require participation by federal legislators. After a compromised election, the states can enforce a tax protest on their own authority, regardless of consent by federal legislators. Tax protests circumvent the entire political process allowing states to set their own agenda and standards for participating in the union. During constitutional crises, only the states have enough organizational capacity and implicit authority to resist an authoritarian occupying federal office.

Although governors may employ tax protests on their own, they should generally only be used when the federal legislature has lawfully shut down all executive agencies. A prolonged government shutdown gives the tax protest its implicit authority, removing many of the risks of incarceration and coordinating the protesting states during the constitutional crisis. When governors act independently, they risk lawful arrest, making it far less likely the succeed. More importantly, when governors act independently, they will lack discipline and coordination, making it easier for the establishment government to isolate and remove them.

It is critically important that the opposition party does not immediately organize an armed response to the authoritarian threat. Peaceable protests have been proven to be more than twice as effective as violent protests. Institutional protests are non-violent in nature, use due process, and are inherently lawful. Without talk of secession, there is only the expectation of concessions, framing the argument as an institutional protest rather than a secession movement. The threat is still implied, but every opportunity is made to negotiate a compromise and an end to the prolonged government shutdown. Secession remains the unspoken alternative if the demands are not met and the authoritarian accepts the inevitability of dissolution.

Institutional protests like tax protests have more innate authority than individual acts because they rely on a great number of persons contributing labors to the effort. As the number of people involved increases, the likelihood of making an error decrease. The large number of participants ensures more perspectives are considered in the deliberation of support. Not only is the wisdom of the crowds harnessed, but the authority is explicit, regardless of the defects in the argument. There is a another more important advantage, more stakeholders mean there are more opportunities for negotiated compromises, minimizing the risk of permanent shutdown and dissolution, making the institutional protest more legitimate and safer for the nation.

A prolonged shutdown is premised an extended time frame permitting more chances for reconciliation and coordination. A shutdown with a length of a few weeks or months, gives all concerned parties enough time to continue negotiating until agreement is reached. During this time, the political parties will also be entrenched in court cases and local elections. The prolonged government shutdown will be priced into elections and the party with higher turnout can dictate outcomes. After elections, the parties negotiating terms may change, producing more pathways to resolution. When institutional protests remain peaceful and organized, it gives the nation every opportunity to resolve their differences through debate, court decisions, elections, and public policy.

Support from a large number of elected representatives provides legitimacy and authority, but enforcing the shutdown will fall to the states and their ability to pass their own laws making it illegal for the federal government to collect revenues when lawfully shutdown. Tax protests focus specifically on tax collection and law enforcement activities that should be expressly forbidden during a government shutdown. When enacted correctly, state governments divert revenues intended for the federal government to their own treasuries by targeting firms doing business within the state or individuals residing in the state. Two goals are accomplished; the federal government is denied revenues while the states acquire new revenues.

After declaring the federal government's actions unconstitutional, the states can make it illegal for companies to remit the income, payroll, and capital gains taxes to the federal government. Targeting firms is a much more efficient use of labor and resources than targeting individuals, considering they aggregate tax liabilities for all of their employees in addition to their own corporate profits. States can drill down to a small group of people making remittance decisions that include employees, vendors, and owners. Threatening corporations with severe fines should be more effective than persecuting individual employees. Companies will already at risk of bankruptcy by the economic consequences of a default or prolonged shutdown and additional fines could force them to dissolve or reorganize. More importantly, fines aren't subject to double taxation laws and couldn't easily be challenged by firms in the court system.

States can incentivize firm compliance by indemnifying corporations from unpaid federal tax liabilities while a lawful shutdown is enforced. State governments will agree to pay the entire federal tax liability should it come due after the conflict ends, eliminating the financial risk for companies. Most corporations will immediately make a cost benefit analysis and correctly decide to withhold payroll, sales, and income taxes from the federal government. By complying with the states' tax protest, firms also avoid heavy fines while earning indemnity from any future federal tax liability. These financial incentives will increase voluntary participation, reducing costs of enforcement, thus improving revenues for the state while denying resources to the federal government.

At the conclusion of the tax-holiday, the corporations will be held harmless with the state responsible for paying back the federal taxes withheld. If the institutional protest is effective, the current administration will make the necessary concessions to reopen the government, and the money collected by the states can be immediately returned to the federal government. When war is avoided, none of the money is spent making it immediately available to settle the obligations. The only situation where the states must repay the federal tax liabilities after those monies have been spent, is when there is open conflict between the state and the federal government. These liabilities can be discounted against worst case scenarios, where they will likely suffer such extraordinarily severe consequences, that the last thing they need worry about are monetary reparations. Part of the concessions that states can demand from the federal government, is forgiveness of these obligations.

Once the extra-constitutional acts of the federal government are declared illegal, the protesting states can pursue economic sanctions against the agencies and principals within the federal government. Protesting states will be able to garnish the wages and attach the assets of principals in the authoritarian regime, allowing them to more forcibly negotiate regime change and reforms with the establishment government. If compromise is reached, the assets can be returned. If the negotiations result in conflict, the assets can be liquidated in order to raise revenues for the war effort. Banks tend to cooperate with the governments who have a more proximate and immediate authority over their individual branch locations. Therefore, most banks will abide by all laws passed by the states, fearing their incorporations might be suspended or assets confiscated by the rebel governments.

Any company selling equipment to the federal government in express disregard of a lack of appropriations and borrowing authority will be assessed for monetary penalties with executives subject to prosecution. Most durable products use parts and supplies by a supply line that crosses multiple state-lines. If just one of those states shut down the production process, the entire supply chain will break down and the durable product can't be manufactured. What remains on their balance sheet will be susceptible to breakdown when parts, munitions, and fuel are in short supply. When supply chains are disrupted and military production is stalled, the federal government won't be able to sustain a long protracted civil war.

Institutional protests overwhelmingly favor the more urban and wealthier states. In the U.S. the Democratic states provide 57% of the federal tax revenues and only receive 50% of the federal subsidies86. If they were to withhold revenues from the federal government, they would effectively cripple the government's ability to suppress protestors with law enforcement or deploy a standing army. During emergencies, expenditures are expected to rise sharply, despite revenues being reduced to just 43% of their former level, with no opportunity to borrow the difference. If peacetime military obligations were 60% of the discretionary budget, the current administration immediately finds itself in 35.2% deficit87. Even if new wartime expenditures only increase spending by 20%, the establishment party could only expect to meet 47.4% of their obligations, after suspending discretionary sector spending.

Federal tax subsidies of 7% are equivalent of nearly 1.4% of GDP using an aggregate federal tax rate of about 20%88. Republican states would lose this amount every year the Democratic states were protesting. In normal years, GDP growth is roughly equal to 2-3%, making the loss of stimulus nearly half of all economic growth in the region89. This loss in GDP is equal to nearly $300B a year for an economy worth $21.43T, which is also equivalent to slightly less than a third of the U.S. federal military budget90. The numbers look even worse when limiting GDP to the states that regularly vote Republican. The missing $300B is more than 3% of their new

---

[86] Internal Revenue Service, " Data Book, 2017", Internal Revenue Service, Publication 55B, March 2018, page 11-13.

[87] Estimate from multiplying 61% x 43% then subtracting the product from the original 61% of the budget.

[88] Johnathan Gruber, "Public Finance and Public Policy". (New York: Worth Publishers, 2013), page 11.

[89] World Bank, "GDP Growth (Annual %) - United States", World Bank, accessed 8/5/2020, retrieved from https://data.worldbank.org/indicator/-NY.GDP.MKTP.KD.ZG?locations=US

[90] World Bank, "GDP (Current US$)- United States", Wolrd Bank, accessed 8/5/2020, retrieved from https://data.worldbank.org/indicator/NY.GDP.MKTP.CD?locations=US

$9.2T GDP tally which is greater than the historic GDP growth rate from the last few decades. If defense budgets are proportional to GDP, the Republican states would lose access to revenues equal to nearly 75% of the new $431B defense budget91.

The Union benefits some states more than the other states. The Republican states are used to receiving 50% of the total federal subsides despite only contributing 43% of the federal revenues. Losing this stimulus results in 16.2% less economic activity in the confederacy, producing a feedback loop towards lower government state tax revenues and worse economic activity92. The new nation will likely suffer several years of economic contractions until their adjusted revenues and expenditures are proportional to their new lower GDP. Under these conditions, private banks might discriminate against their government debt in favor of more secure investments, like those in the Democratic states.

A tax protest by the Democratic states would free up an additional 12.3% of economic activity within their states, improving state tax revenues by 2.4% of GDP93. The additional $300B could easily subsidized a war effort against a destabilized and defunded confederacy. Confidence is critical when organizing a resistance movement and preparing to wage war; the states with sounder public finance systems will inspire more courage in the citizenry, and more support from the banks which are needed to fund the effort. Democratic states will also have sounder balance sheets after the split, making it much more likely they repay obligations accrued during the crisis, making it more likely allied states and banks loan them money.

Payroll tax remittances require special attention during a tax protest. One of the first acts of protesting states should be to establish a pension system to replace the federal system.

---

[91] Kimberly Amadeo, "Current US Federal Government Spending", The Balance, Updated Jun 28th, 2020, retrieved from https://www.the-balance.com/current-u-s-federal-government-spending-3305763
[92] Estimated from multiplying 43% by the 7% difference in federal tax subsidies in combined economy.
[93] Estimated from multiplying 57% by the 7% difference in federal tax subsidies in combined economy.

Pensions systems typically invests surplus revenues in government treasuries to earn a secure return at a low stipulated rate. When the pension system buys treasuries, it produces a stable revenue stream for the government to rely on. Payroll taxes are often nearly 1/5th of all mandatory spending resulting in one of the most secure sources of emergency war-time borrowing, one that is not susceptible to market collapses in the bond markets. Deficit financing still requires legitimate appropriation and borrowing authority to act on, but the individual states are more likely to be able to continue passing laws and budgets.

Protesting states will benefit more from the purchase of government debt as they have no established credit in the international system of finance. Ordinarily, they would pay huge financing costs on bonds to wage a war for regime change, independence, or secession, but the pension system allows the government to dictate the return paid on the instruments, sidestepping what could be a movement-crushing obligation. Protesting states will need to operate in an environment of debt default threats, government shutdowns, and economic recessions making them dependent on the more predictable revenues and obligations provided by nation pensions and retirement systems.

Likewise, establishment states are also dependent on war financing during wars of succession and secession. The current administration will continue to rely on payroll taxes to provide a revenue that is immune to disruptions in the secondary bond market. They can use surplus pension revenues to offset the costs of a war when those proceeds are used to purchase government debt. With the dedicated source of deficit financing, the establishment states can improve their ability to rebuke the protesting states and preserve the current democratic administration. Their appropriations may be unlawful, but the revenue streams will not be susceptible to disruptions in the bond markets.

Most developed nations provide their citizens a pension or retirement system so most nations can benefit from similar policies. The United States Social Security system provides an excellent example of how critical pension systems are during crises. Current Social Security revenues are 23% of the

U.S. total budget with a dollar amount is roughly equal to $1,150B a year in revenues94 95. These costs are paid almost entirely by payroll taxes split between individuals and firms. When the revenues come in, they are immediately used to pay short-term pension liabilities and the excess is used to purchase special U.S. Treasuries providing a stipulated rate of return96. Over the last few decades, the Social Security Trust has accumulated nearly $2,800B in assets97 but the fund is expected to start drawing down its reserve of U.S. Treasuries now that the pension liability is greater than the payroll tax revenues.

After the Social Security Trust is exhausted, there will be an approximate gap of 21% between revenues and expenditures in the pension system, so any fix will need to exceed this amount before contributing any excess financing for emergencies and wars98. The first policy an administration should pursue is increasing the payroll taxes paid by both employers and employees. Even a modest change in the rate will produce significant improvements in war financing. For example, if total payroll taxes were increased by 3.825% or just 1.91% for employees and 1.91% for employers, it would capture nearly $287.5B in extra revenues. This is nearly twice the annual cost for the Iraq War which averaged more than $125B/year for the first 7 years99.

---

[94] Center on Budget and Policy Priorities, "Policy Basics: Where Do Our Federal Tax Dollars Go?", Center on Budget and Policy Priorities, Updated April 9, 2020, retrieved from https://www.cbpp.org/research/federal-budget/policy-basics-where-do-our-federal-tax-dollars-go.
[95] Kimberly Amadeo, "Current Federal Mandatory Spending", The Balance, Updated March 3, 2020, retrieved from https://www.thebalance.com/current-federal-mandatory-spending-3305772.
[96] David Pattison, "Social Security Trust Fund Cash Flows and Reserves", Social Security Administration, Social Security Bulletin, Vol 75, No 1, 2015, retrieved from https://www.ssa.gov/policy/docs/ssb/v75n1/v75n1p1.html.
[97] David Pattison, "Social Security Trust Fund Cash Flows and Reserves", Social Security Administration, Social Security Bulletin, Vol 75, No 1, 2015, retrieved from https://www.ssa.gov/policy/docs/ssb/v75n1/v75n1p1.html.
[98] Steven Goldstein, "Social Security costs to exceed revenue next year, trustee report shows", MarketWatch, April 22, 2019, retrieved from https://www.marketwatch.com/story/social-security-costs-to-exceed-revenue-next-year-trustee-report-shows-2019-04-22.
[99] Kimberly Amadeo, "Cost of Iraq War, Its Timeline, and the Economic Impact", The Balance, Updated July 15, 2020, retrieved from

The government must also to uncap the income threshold on payroll taxes. Currently, payroll taxes only apply on incomes less than $137,700100. However, most of the growth in incomes have occurred in high-income groups, and more specifically the top 5% of all income-earners101. This group saw wage increases of 41% with the majority of those gains being excluded from social security taxes102. Uncapping the income threshold could accommodate between 25% and 90% of the 21% deficit between revenues and obligations103. If the $1,150B benchmark is used, the new tax would roughly translate to nearly $217B in protected revenues.

Another critical intervention is raising the minimum wage to $15.00. Approximately 19% of U.S. workers make less than $12.50/hour104. Slightly more than that many would benefit from a raise to $15.00/hour. Raising wages in the 1st income quartile will only have a modest positive effect on raising social security revenues but this is still meaningful to a nation in crisis. The average of 40% improvement in wages will translate to a much larger base for both the employer and employee payroll taxes. Even if this only improves the Social Security revenues by just 5% of the $1,150B figure that would

---

https://www.thebalance.com/cost-of-iraq-war-timeline-economic-impact-3306301.

[100] Social Security Resource Center, "What is the maximum amount of income that is subject to FICA taxes?" AARP, accessed on July 11, 2020, Retrieved from https://www.aarp.org/retirement/social-security/questions-answers/maximum-amount-income-subject-to-fica-tax/.

[101] Juliana Menasce Horowitz, Ruth Iglienik, and Rakesh Kochhar, "Trends in income and wealth inequality", Pew Research Center, Jan 9, 2020, retrieved from https://www.pewsocialtrends.org/2020/01/09/trends-in-income-and-wealth-inequality/.

[102] Lawrence Mishel, Elise Gould, and Josh Bivens, "Wage Stagnation in Nine Charts", Economic Policy Institute, Jan 6, 2015, retrieved from https://www.epi.org/publication/charting-wage-stagnation/.

[103] Kathleen Romig, "Increasing Payroll Taxes Would Strengthen Social Security", Center on Budget and Policy Priorities, September 27, 2016, Center on Budget and Policy Priorities, retrieved from https://www.cbpp.org/-research/social-security/increasing-payroll-taxes-would-strengthen-social-security

[104] Steven Goldstein, "A majority of Americans make less than $20 per hour", MarketWatch, Nov 17, 2014, retrieved from https://www.marketwatch.com/story/a-majority-of-americans-make-less-than-20-per-hour-2014-11-14.

be nearly $58B a year in protected off budget war financing. A call to raise wages will increase support for the administration proposing the changes in the segment of the population most likely to be conscripted into the war effort. This should soften resistance against the protesting states or sure up support among loyalist states.

There is a significant monetary reward for occupying the federal executive branch when secession threatens the union. If half the nation's citizens reside in seceding states, half of the obligations incurred by the national pension system are available for repayment of obligations incurred resulting from the war. In the United States, this means nearly half of the $2,800B in assets may be available to pay off the debt accumulated during the prosecution of the war effort. The seceding states will not have a claim to the assets if they used violence to separate themselves. The portfolio is roughly equivalent to more than 11 years of war financing at the $125B/year cost for the Iraq War or $500B/year worth of war financing for a war lasting only 3 years.

Protesting states can focus on developing their own pension systems because most of the payroll taxes are collected by firms residing within their jurisdictions. If the states are already targeting firms for other income and profits taxes, they can easily divert payroll taxes to a new pension system. The funds are not spent directly, allowing them to be repatriated into the national pension system after the conflict is resolved. Combined, these reforms add nearly $650Bin new revenues. Although only national numbers are examined, they can easily be adjusted by partisan affiliation for net revenues gained. The Democratic states control 57% of the GDP which suggests they will recover 57% of the payroll tax revenues, roughly equating to roughly $322B. The Republican can only expect 43% of payroll taxes, for $243B.

These payroll tax revenues are in addition to the regular income and profits tax revenues, expected to be diverted; the Democrats can expect a swing of more than $622B additional tax revenues, while Republicans see a loss of $50B. It there was ever conflict between the states, the Democratic states would have significant advantage in either position, as the establishment trying to protect the union, or as protesting states shaking off an authoritarian takeover of the nation. The Iraq war cost an average of $100/year, with a population of 25m, suggesting the Democrats could subsidize a war effort 6x as intense, covering 150m, without taking on any extraordinary borrowing. More importantly, the Republicans will immediately put on a clock, losing huge sums of money, with no expectations of being able to sustain a large protracted war, making them more likely to sue or peace or surrender.

Tax protests are an important backstop to the other institutional protests available to the states, justifying the development of the policies prior to a conflict. When civil servants have expertise in the public finance, supply chains, and due process, they can make better predictions and respond much more quickly to threats. If states are reluctant to develop these emergency plans, they are more likely to be taken advantage of. Without robust emergency preparedness, there is no way the states can discourage misbehavior during elections, or authoritarian abuses during office.

Tax protests allow states to enforce the lawful shutdowns agreed to in the federal government. All institutional protests are tacitly agreed to by the parties in office; the terms are clearly detailed out and agreement will end the standoff. The consequences are spelled out in the language of an institutional protest; the parties publicly declaring their readiness to accept dissolution or regime change. If the parties did not agree with the results, they would have moderated their positions. The states are merely carrying out the terms of the contract by diverting income, profit, and payroll taxes back to the states.

It is important for states to reject an authoritarian takeover through a coup or compromised election. The more numerous the states collaborating in resistance, the larger portion of the economy under rebel control, and a larger population to draw on for labor. Capturing a significant portion of GDP opens a host of other nonviolent interventions to coerce the authoritarian states back to democracy or back into the Union. Democratic states can impose economic sanctions on principals and firms supporting the authoritarian regime. Causing economic harm does more than incite their public into rebellion. It creates incentives for the authoritarian states to pass laws protecting civil rights and limited voting rights. Economic sanctions are movable and negotiable, creating a moving average that can quickly adapt to new players and new conditions. If states do not reject an authoritarian regime, they will not be able to influence the regime at all. If the states collaborate with the regime, they can't discourage other dilapidations in the quality of elections or representation.

In the United States. nearly 60% of the GDP is controlled in Democratic states. Economic sanctions by Democratic governors would be a far more effective strategy to influence authoritarians in formerly Republican states. Not only would firms need to maintain open supply chains with Democratic states, but many of the principals would see their wealth rapidly deteriorate when assets become inaccessible and non-fungible. Republican states could not effectively leverage economic sanctions while controlling only 40% of the nation's GDP. If the Democratic states hesitate, choosing to remain in the Union, they will lose access to any authority to impose economic sanctions. If the Democratic states collaborate, they will permit the authoritarian regime to leverage the entire GDP of the nation towards policing and surveillance powers. Without any economic disruptions, the authoritarian regime could divert huge sums of money into the military and intelligence agencies to continue suppressing the formerly democratic populations.

As scorched earth policy with conflate the losses in federalist tax policies with an inability to trade with 57% of the combined economy, with levies and garnishments on assets of principles supporting the authoritarian regime. Access to capital through banks can be limited through sanctions and trade policy. Access to the ports and international trade can be limited by sanctions and embargos. Liberal immigration policies in free states (democratic states) can rob the authoritarians of important labor supplies and consumption. The 43% of GDP could shrink by significant amounts every year the states resist civil rights reforms and high-quality democratic entitlements. The states would immediately lose 20% of their structural financing from federal subsidies making it unlikely banks and other nations support their deficit financing through sovereign debt.

The combined effect of the economic contraction and public finance disruption should make them pliable to reunification or reform, only made possible by coordinated embargos and sanctions from the formerly allied democratic states. When the formerly Republican states suffer excessive public finance crises, resulting from the loss of the federalist tax subsidies, a destabilized currency following economic sanctions could completely up-end their ability to borrow or spend their way out of a recession, or support the police and military spending to preserve a surveillance state. The proportion of GDP between the democratic states and authoritarian states, would widen dramatically from 57/43% to 70/30% or more after adjusting the GDP controlled by despots for new currency valuations, new trade flows, and new levels of taxation compensating for the loss of federalist subsidies, increased military spending, and welfare from the sharp declines in economy.

When the authoritarian firms risk excessive losses in profits and wealth, they will be far more likely to support regime change in authoritarian states. The sooner this happens the better, as most of the public will still have preferences for democracy. The longer the democratic states wait to secede or imposes economic sanctions, the more likely the population adapts their culture and behavior to the new expectations. There should be no doubt, that minority populations caught behind enemy lines after a successful secession or coup, are much better off if the Democratic states separate themselves and are able to effectively organize interventions through economic sanctions and a threat of military invasion, then if the Democratic states hesitate and collaborate, thinking an authoritarian regime can be coerced back to democracy by protestors alone. An authoritarian United States is a nuclear power, and no other democratic state will be able to risk military invasion. An authoritarian United States also remains an economic superpower and won't likely be subjected to economic sanctions by other parties, especially if most of the world's largest economic partners are authoritarian and not democratic.

Congress members will have to demonstrate leadership and pursue threats of debt defaults and government shutdowns as course corrections, backstopped by governors with access to their state militias, if nonviolent strategies fail and armed insurrection is necessary to prevent an authoritarian takeover. Governors will have to rely on tax protests to prevent an authoritarian in federal office from consolidating power through the military and domestic intelligence agencies and use trade embargoes and economic sanctions to coerce the confederate states back to democracy afterward. The proliferation of nuclear weapons makes an outbreak of violence less likely, which places more emphasis on strategic non-violent strategies like coordinated protests, debt defaults, government shutdowns, tax protests, and economic sanctions as the primary movers towards reform and reunification.

8 GUARDING THE NATION

It is undeniable that sovereign states have the authority to deploy armed militias and law enforcement to secure their own territories and rights. This is much different than an individual's right to bear arms. An individual may own weapons but has no outright authority to use them unless their home is directly threatened by criminal acts. An individual's right to bear arms does not give them the discretion necessary to deem a government's actions are illicit or an administration illegitimate. Where the individuals rights end, the government's responsibilities start. A duly elected democratic government is charged with protecting and enforcing the individual liberties and rights given to their residents. Only the government has the right to use institutional protests and legally deploy armed resistance against another government. Individual perspectives are lacking in understanding, expertise, and responsibility. They may have great imaginations and sympathies but they simply can't occupy the perspective of another person, of different class, race, or gender. Only electorates have enough collective wisdom to embark in armed rebellion. Even when it is the government acting, the government can't satisfy the demands and expectations of all of their citizens, but they come infinity closer than individuals.

Individuals can take up arms against an authoritarian, but they do so without the implicit support of the electorate or government. Most individuals also lack the training and expertise to effectively resist and authoritarian. More importantly, they may lack the judgment to effectively evaluate the situation and determine which acts are authoritarian and which are simply abusive. Most individuals cannot know for themselves if an election is fraudulent or if the constitution is in violation. Most individuals rely on experts and institutions to give them the credible evidence to come to an appropriate conclusion. When they strike out on their own, they are more likely to harm themselves or innocents. Even the exercise of individual resistance is futile, unless terroristic methods are employed to maximize death and disability. The only natural right the individual has is for resistance is to participate in a municipal, county, or state government which has the authority to rebel. None of this means, an individual can't act to resist and authoritarian, but it does mean they must first submit themselves to the discretion of an elected body able to deliberate and debate on the issues of revolution. Individuals may be delegated authority to take up arms against another government, but it only when there is a consensus of the governed. When no democratic government presently exists, they must create one, to legitimize their action.

There is a natural check against state governments prematurely and illegitimately organizing a rebellion through their state militias. State militias are normally unreliable, subject to state level politics before deployment. It is very unlikely that a single state calls up their national guard and successfully secedes from the union. It is even less likely that half of the state organize themselves into a confederacy to challenge the authority of the federal government. As the numbers of states and voters increase, the probability of an event decreases. The malice may be present but the will is lacking. In order for states to formally declare secession they need the support of both the executives and legislative branches, subjecting the effort to current and future elections. The amount of work needed to lawfully secede will discourage most attempts, promoting security within the union, but when a danger is so obvious and imminent, the public will give implicit consent to raise and state militia and fully fund it.

Within the United States, the National Guard armies are the state militias referenced in the 2nd amendment. States have a Constitutional right to organize them and deploy them when needed. It is a right that should be limited, even more legitimate than the individual right to bear arms. During the colonial period, it was the right and obligation for states to organize militias and most individuals have to furnish their own arms. For that reason, the individual right to bear arms is confounded with the states right to organize militia, but it is misconception to suggest that the individual's right to bear arms can't be regulated. In the modern era, states provide the training and weapons for a fully authorized national guard Army. An individual right to bear arms has absolutely no impact on the state's ability to mobilize a militia, and therefore doesn't support the main intention of the 2nd Amendment. In fact, when individuals act on their own, they are more likely to be classified as terrorists than freedom fighters. Unless individuals submit to a chain of command within a federal armed force or state militia, they will be criminals rather than heroes. Not only are state militias more effective, they are inherently legitimate due to the authority vested in the electorate.

Individuals are better off enlisting in the state militia than continuing as an illicit freedom fighter. Not only will they operate within the bounds of the law, but they will receive the training and equipment necessary to be successful. Individuals relying on their own discretion and weapons actually harm the effectiveness of recruitment drives in the state, creating a counter-revolutionary impediment. Freedom forces be easier to target and neutralize, but they are nearly impossible to coordinate with regular militia. Individuals believing, they will organize themselves outside of a legitimate state or municipal authority will harm the cause. If the public associates the terrorists with the state sponsored resistance movement, they may not support it, risking everybody's natural rights and lives. Their actions will be illegal, ineffective, and counterproductive, weakening the arguments in favor of an individual right to bear arms.

When negotiations fail to move the government towards reform and back to democracy, the states will have to rely on their militias to secure order and protect their constituencies' rights. The most important use of national guard armies is to provide stability and security during the crisis. This naturally requires the state to police their own residents but it also means guarding their principals and representatives. When federal representatives are sent to the capitol to legislate, they must have confidence that they won't be arrested or shot while pursuing impeachment proceeding, government shutdowns, or debt defaults. An authoritarian will be tempted to threaten and cajole individual representatives if they are not protected by law enforcement and militia. An authoritarian could otherwise attempt to put down an institutional protest by incarcerating participating representatives and using the new quorum to pass their anti-democratic laws.

When the authoritarian administration refuses to operate within the bounds of the constitution and expectations of democratic governance, the state militias will give the democrats enough time organize their own standing armies to oppose the wayward government. Militias are generally much smaller than federal armies, they have less expertise and less sophisticated weapons, but they may still be effective enough to delay occupation long enough for the rebels to conscript new enlisted, manufacture new arms, and rally allies to their defense. The authoritarian government likely doesn't have enough enlisted to fully enforce martial law and occupation of the participating states, especially if more than a quarter of the armed forces were composed of state militia from the protesting states. The authoritarian government will need time to conscript recruits, if they can still appropriate funds and borrow, giving the state militias and local police enough protection and time for the rebel states to match the numbers of enlisted and manufacturing normally controlled by the federal military.

The states should all have emergency plans for funding and supplying a militia, including borrowing authority and control over supply chains. Many states have sovereignty, such as those in the United States, which means they have the authority to prepare for situations where the federal government may be compromised by a debt default, government shutdown, a disputed election, or authoritarian coup. The states can look at all scenarios normally excluded when a fully functioning and legitimate federal government typically intervenes, allowing the states to prepare for domestic conflict years ahead of a precipitating event. This planning may benefit confederate states considering secession, but the risk of an authoritarian coup outweigh the risk of a separatist movement in state governments. A declaration for secession will likely be preceded by, or immediately followed by, a threat to default or prolonged government shutdown, passing priority to the loyalist states to respond almost exclusively on the state-level. Those states that developed funding plans and guaranteed supply chains will be better able to support a federal governments whose authority and finances are compromised. If the nation depends exclusively on a federal government which is shutdown or whose debt has been defaulted on, it significantly increases the probability of a successful secession and increased the frequency of attempts.

A small number national guard armies supplemented by an fully equipped and military trained police force should be substantial enough to prevent a quick occupation after a compromised election or coup attempt. The police will know the city or state intimately and have advantages navigating the territory or pulling resources from it. Local officials may find it easier to rapidly expand the police force instead of bulking up military enlisted which require specialized training in bases far away from the state. Civilians are much more likely to join a local police force to protect their immediate neighborhoods, than enlist in an army that could send them hundreds or thousands of miles away. Cities and counties can act independently of a state or federal executive, allowing for a more rapid expansion of budgetary line items devoted to defense personnel and armaments. T

The national guard units and scaled up police force should discourage incursion or occupation long enough for the states to raise a fully financed and armed standing army. The combined size of a police force and national guard contingent should equal the size of a standing army diminished by the loss of the defecting state militia. When the states protest the outcome of the election, they should immediately coordinate with the federal legislators for a prolonged government shutdown and debt default. Both of these institutional protests could cause significant loyalty shifts in enlisted, causing a sharp decline in the federal military while rapidly increasing the number of state militia.

States and cities have an incredible advantage over their federal counterparts when marshalling their militias to resist authoritarian government. All of their troops are locally sourced. There are far fewer issues of loyalty. The enlisted were often born in the state they are charged with protecting. Their families still live there. All of their friends depend on them to remain honest and faithful to the state. This is not true for federal forces which draw enlisted from every state and deploy them to states without regard to former residence. Federal enlisted may rethink their allegiance to the authoritarian government if it is in breach of the oaths taken during enlistment. The leadership may still support the administration but many of the enlisted and their immediate officers will have reservations. Federal forces will have far more defections than state militias, negatively impacting their effectiveness when deployed to states as an occupying force.

Special importance should be given to base location and armories, especially if large portions of enlisted defect with officers and senior level commanders. Rebel states could capture bases and capitol ships through the declarations of independence followed by loyalty shifts from institutional protests. The defection of just one air force base or capitol ship with nuclear weapons could end a conflict and coerce a negotiated settlement. Bases are typically situated in states which may be hostile to a regime and capitol ship are often at sea and under the rigid command of a single officer, exposing an implicit opportunity for rebels, be they confederates or democrats. Of course, the strategic value of a nuclear weapon is only worth as much as the intent behind the threat to use it, with authoritarians much more likely to deploy the weapons on their own people (from formerly allied states) than a democratic regime, which would otherwise suffer terrible electoral consequences for the threat and use of overwhelming force.

States benefit from having more proximate control over the companies operating within their regions. The capitol could he hundreds of miles away, maybe thousands, causing companies to defer more to the state's regulatory and taxing authority. States can more easily impose tax protests and disrupt federal revenues. More importantly, they can interdict the supply chain for federal munitions and durable products. States can make it illegal to supply and arm the federal forces, which are heavily dependent on supply chains crossing through several adversarial states. States are not subject to this threat and can rely on more readily available small arms and local produced munitions. When necessary, the state militias can raid the abandoned or short-staffed federal bases to appropriate the weapons caches. If there are any holes in their supply chains, and a lack of durable products.

One of the biggest obstacles to a rapid deployment of forces on the state level are borrowing constraints and budgetary limits. Both states and cities should have emergency plans to implement tax protests to deny an authoritarian or confederate government the revenues they need to fund their operations. Corporations are aggregators for profits, personal withholding for income taxes, and payroll taxes, making them easier targets for disruption. Cities and states can quickly pass laws making it illegal to support an authoritarian or confederate governments, allowing them to coerce participation through economic sanctions or a threat of incarceration. Balanced budget amendments should also be suspended during war-time, so that the states can compensate for a diminished capacity within the federal government. Cities don't usually have balanced budget amendments, allowing them to take on debt uninhibited, but they have less revenues and assets.

Deferring to municipal and city executives for a scaled increase in combatants also introduces the possibility of improving armed resistance within confederate or enemy states. If a secession is declared by executives, mayors from within those states can resist by relying on their police forces, and rapidly expanding them to aid allies. Cities are often are more diverse than rural communities, command substantial portions of the population, control significant resources, and have budgetary powers that may not be constrained by balanced budget amendments. Leveraging cities after a coup attempt may be the best way to rapidly deploy counter-authoritarian forces in both allied and confederate territories. They can be integral components of a supply chain behind enemy lines, saboteurs, and freedom fighters. Free cities can be a money suck for authoritarian regimes trying to suppress resistance, especially if the other states organize an armed response on their borders. However, cities are not sovereign powers like states, and therefore have fewer rights and a diminished authority to plan or prepare for resisting a state government or authoritarian federal government. States should prepare to export their plans to allied cities within confederate states, when the federal government is prevented from acting with initiative.

States can also reach out to the legislators in other states to organize their own coordinated resistance through debt defaults and government shutdowns. Without budget appropriation authority states will not be able to mount a durable defense against free cities or the militias from other states. Many of the states will have split legislatures, with executives from one party and legislators from another, making any real coordinated effort impossible, with an increased chance of default or shutdown. Current law enforcement expenditures only go so far, and with balanced budget amendments and a stoppage to all new expenditures, any state assistance to a federal government that is hobbled by a debt default or shutdown of their own should be minimal. Although debt defaults are harder to impose on state governments, if given enough time, and with the right opportunity, they can also impose bankruptcy on a hostile executive branch allying with an authoritarian regime or separatist movement.

States can collect information on the due process of other states and look at it for weaknesses that can be exploited in an emergency. They will also want to look at allied states to estimate the odds of their succumbing to a default or shutdown. Every state government should be analyzing intelligence on social and political movements around the support for institutional protests, and how consequential they may be to a resistance movement. Allied states will need to gauge their own ability to marshal budgetary, labor, and supplies from other states, and many of these assets are constrained by due process and attitudes of politicians in other state government. Periods on instability can last years, terms, or decades, and state executives should have an eye on where their national guard armies are deployed, and how institutional protests can be deployed within authoritarian states. A well times institutional protest on a state-level could seriously impair a resistance movement or an authoritarian occupations, so executives must be guarded against and ready to deploy such strategies in an emergency period.

It is not advisable that state governments take up arms against an authoritarian government before shutting it down and crippling its finances. Armed resistance is much easier to deploy when the federal government has defaulted on its debts, lacking appropriations authority due to a shutdown, or lacking revenues after a tax protest, making the principle use of the state militia to protect the governors and representatives imposing the institutional protests. However, sometimes the choices are made for us and an optimal outcome is not possible. In an emergency, the state governments must be aware of the limits of their own authority and which strategies will be most effective. At the very least, the state governments should impose a tax protest to divert revenues at the source, and then mobilize their national guard in order to preserve their sovereignty and territorial boundaries.

Depending on which states have trifectas, and which states continue supporting the establishment party, even more states may withhold their national guard armies from deployment. The immediate deployment of 25% of the armed forces, may be enough to discourage a federal government that only has access to 50% of frontline combat troops and no reliable way to pay them. In the United States, the Constitution expressly forbids federal enlisted from being used during domestic emergencies, which may cause more states to rally to the opposition party, and evens the field between the authoritarian federal government and the free states, if they remain in the Union. Estimates can be made beforehand, but after a precipitating event occurs, the quickly changing landscape could present more opportunities and more risk, as populations and governments test loyalties and legal boundaries.

As long as the state militia is used defensively there shouldn't be any legal challenges or implied threat of coup when they are called up for service amidst a domestic row. It would be questionable if the protesting states called up their state militia with the intent to occupy other states, but if they restrain the movements of the militia to their own territory, there should be no legal or moral obstacles. It would then be on the federal government to diffuse the situation by limiting their law enforcement or military operations within those jurisdictions. A defensive posture declares intent while still remaining unconfrontational. If all governments are meeting expectations and abiding by the constitution, a defensive posture won't have any long-term consequences other than costs. Precautions can be taken, without being overly provocative, helping to diffuse the dangerous situation.

If the opposition party has access to their state militias during the event, and they are uniform in their dispositions, they can call them up, denying the establishment party a significant portion of their total army, depending on how the armed forces are organized. The federal government should immediately recognize their diminished capacity and reconsider their offending position. In the United States, the national guard represent nearly 50% of all the frontline troops, and it is frontline combat troops that are needed to occupy and hold territory. If half of the states defect from the Union, they will deny the federal government 25% of their total armed forces even before appropriations powers are withheld, and payroll stoppages force the remaining enlisted to seek employment by the state and municipal governments.

Purposefully organizing foreign deployments of an opposition parties National Guard Armies during Presidential election years is the most effective way to quash rebellion after installing an executive after a compromised election. In the case of the United States, National Guard Armies represent 50% of the total frontline combat troops in the Army. When the executive branch sends a deployment made up of mostly or exclusively opposition party enlisted, it could deny the opposition party nearly 20% their total forces during a conflict, discouraging their fulminations and preventing them from organizing a protest. The opposition party will take stock of their missing enlisted only after an imminent threat is recognized, either not being aware of the deployments before that moment, or being naïve on their usefulness during a conflict.

When national guard units are sent overseas near election transition years, it denies the opposition party an opportunity to challenge the outcome of a compromised election. Courage is a scarce commodity, and if the opposition party only occupies 20 of the 50 states, it is already nearly impossible to coordinate a response focused on calling up the national guard in preparation for armed resistance. Executives will tend to hesitate before calling their militias to arms making abusive deployments very effective measures to quell protests. If 20% of these units are sent overseas by a hostile federal executive, it could immediately cool any momentum for rebellion by the states, regardless of the quality or legitimacy of the election.

If the largest and most capable states don't have access to their national guard, the other states would likely balk at the chance to defend their democratic entitlements. Even if they exhibited courage, with 20% or more of their armed forces missing, the protest may lack the necessary support to succeed. Relocating opposition party national guard units to overseas deployments is a clear indication of the probability a coup occurs after a compromised election. State executives should watch troop movements closely, because they can also be called up to guard the border or for some other domestic use, and still be a means to deny the states their militias during an event.

The Democrats should view the unilateral deployment of Democratic National Guard units overseas during the 2005 Presidential election transition year as another attempted Coup. Republicans sent a deployment comprised exclusively of Democratic enlisted overseas in the year following the Presidential year with the express intent of putting down a Democratic protest if the Presidential election was compromised for a second time, noting the Supreme Court intervened in 2000 and ruled in their favor. The year following a Presidential election year is more important as it is the year one administration transitions to another. The 2005 National Guard deployment represented nearly 20% of those states that reliably vote Democratic and it would have hamstrung any Democratic response, forcing them to accept any terms offered by the republicans.

The policy wasn't just the result of a single wrong decision. They all went along with it. The military leadership, the Congressional leadership and the administration. None of the officials questioned the highly partisan and dangerous decision to isolate the Democratic states and send only their National Guard Armies overseas during Presidential Election years. There can be no doubt they understood the implications and the consequences. The Democrats must quickly learn the lessons of the past and resist and war with Venezuela or Iran that might be an opportunity for Trump to send Democratic National Guard Armies overseas.

It has been demonstrated that the Republicans are willing to start a war just prior to a Presidential election, with the express intent of removing Democratic National Guard Armies from the domestic theatre. The 2003 Iraq War enabled Republicans to plan and send the Democratic National Guard Armies overseas during the year of regime change and the 2019 Iraq deployment accomplishes the same goal. The Republicans are currently discussing sending 120,000 soldiers to Iraq in 2019 which is nearly equivalent to the 140,000 soldiers sent to Iraq in 2003. The Democrats should be carefully watching to see if the Republicans plan to send their National Guard Armies overseas during the Presidential election year 2020 and the transition in 2021. Democrats can't trust Republican administrations to engineer deployment schedules during times of war. This is the single biggest threat to world stability. The United States is no longer able to organize and mobilize their combined military force to intervene in world events without a large portion of the Representatives fearing abuse or usurpation. This will embolden our enemies in the world and increase the likelihood of conflict.

This is a devastating blow to U.S. war readiness. The Democrats should be hesitant before letting a Republican President send them overseas. There was malice behind the deployments. They were intended to exploit the trust of the democrats. The deployments can be used to force the Democrats to surrender or accept terms they otherwise wouldn't during a crisis. Make no mistake, there were deaths of National Guard enlisted during those time frames and the blame falls squarely on the Republicans. There is always the risk of death during enlistment, but in return the enlisted expect their neighbors, families, and friends to be more secure after deployment. They don't expect their courage and sacrifice to be used to weaken their respective states and expose their communities' members to political, violence or worse. It must be understood that, in any normal rotation, an equal number of armies from both parties would be deployed, and the burden and risk of death with be distributed evenly between Republicans and Democrats. This trust was violated and the Democrat should expect to be abused again, and again, until the deployments are regulated and fully transparent. As it stands now, the Democrats can't trust the Republicans to start another war and then deploy Democratic enlisted overseas while there is risk of another political deployment and domestic political instability.

Prior to 2011 and Democratic intervention, all National Guard deployment schedules were public, displayed in Congressional Records (CRS), the Stars and Stripes magazine, and covered by the Media. Prior to 2011, the minority party and governors could openly and legally view the deployment schedules and challenge their fairness or legitimacy. When the Democrats in office decided to classify the deployment process and cover up the indiscretions of the Republicans, they created a precedent where future National Guard Deployments are classified and the Democratic governors won't be able to evaluate the risk of agreeing to the terms. Worse, Democrats have never resisted a National Guard Deployment so they are more than likely to submit to the opaque process rather than question it.

When the Democrats in Office classified the 2005 and 2009 National Guard deployment schedules, they created an obstacle for their own representatives to discuss the abusive use of deployments with the public. The Democrats may find themselves a minority in Congress again, with no authority to resist similar deployment schedules. When governors are unable to coordinate with other governors to evaluate the deployments, and there is no precedent for resisting them, the nation is exposed to risks of usurpation with no recourse to prevent it. Democrats should have realized the risks back in 2011 when they were reminded of the partisan National Guard deployments during the political crisis over the debt ceiling and Sequestration Act. The Democrats should not have tried avoiding conflict by covering up the dangerous Republican behavior, instead of seeking to regulate it and win elections with a public rebuke of the behavior.

The states have rights, especially those guaranteed by the 2nd amendment to organize a well-regulated militia, and those of other sovereign powers established by the federalism clause. This extends to the discretion of when governors agree to send their National Guards overseas for deployment. If they feel there is too much risk, they have the authority to withhold them. The present environment of debt defaults, government shutdowns, compromised presidential elections, and the prior history of abuse, casts doubt in the safety of deploying National Guards overseas during presidential election years. If there were reforms to ensure that the National Guard could not be abused with political deployments, it would go a long way to mitigate concerns. No National Guard deployment should ever be classified as secret as it pertains specifically to the safety and security of certain states, not other stats or the federal government. This has not occurred and the conditions are getting more partisan and more dangerous. Therefore, the Democratic governors should assert their rights over the National Guard and keep them state-side during the year of the Presidential election and the year of transition.

It is clear that the Republican administration was preparing to quell to protests from the Democratic states if there was a compromised election in 2004 and 2008. It is also evident that the Republican Party will support candidates refusing to accept the outcomes of Presidential elections they lose, while accepting Senatorial and Congressional elections they win. Nearly 77% of the Republican Party believes the election was fraudulent, and 66% believe President Biden is illegitimate[105]. Supporters in Texas have even suggested armed rebellion to overturn the election. President Trump refused to concede the election and made the unprecedented decision to leverage his Supreme Court and circuit court appoint what to intervene in the election by lawsuits. Once again, it's the attempt that is important, rather than the outcome. Although the Republican administration in 2000 was appointed by the Supreme Court, there was no conflict in 2004. The reason there was no contested election is purely due to the Democrats not challenging the outcome. If they had, the Republican had already prepared a coup, to quickly put down their protests.

Sometimes the trend lines are more important than the local outcomes. Although, there was no compromised election in 2004 to necessitate the use of violence against the Democratic state. If the Republicans are willing to commit to these overt acts of abuse, they clearly don't fear the consequences of being discovered. This behavior is evidence of an agenda outside of the current democratic paradigm. They are taking risks to achieve these goals, suggesting there will be other attempts. Although the Trump administration is likely to leave office in 2021, his challenge of true validity of the election is producing a culture of mistrust in democracy. They may not have acted on it, but they did create the conditions where a future candidate or administration could challenge the outcome. The methods are already present, they are simply waiting for the opportunity.

Even more concerning are the reoccurring threats of default and government shutdown, which generally follow a Democratic election to office. Threats of debt defaults are not common in any country other than the United States. Frequent and severe government shutdowns are not normally found in democracies other than United States. The Republicans are using Cost Benefit Analyses and coming to the conclusion that destroying the federal government is an acceptable outcome if their demands are not met. If the consequences of a default are

---

[105] Christopher Keating, "Quinnipiac Poll: 77% of Republicans believe there was widespread fraud in the presidential election; 60% overall consider Joe Biden's victory legitimate", Hartford Courant, Dec 10, 2020, Retrieved from https://www.courant.com/politics/hc-pol-q-poll-republicans-believe-fraud-20201210-pcie3uqqvrhyvnt7geohhsyepe-story.html

not acceptable, then using them as negotiating tools diminishes in utility. If the threat of default was not real, the use of them during negotiations would not be respected, reducing their effectiveness. The prolonged government shutdown is public acknowledgment that democracy is voluntary. The shut downs are intended to remind the Democratic administration how fragile the democracy is, and how easily it is to organize a resistance. Government shutdowns and threats of default are shots across the bow of the ship. They are warning shots that elections have consequences and the opposition party has alternative options to the union.

When one looks at the trend lines and not the outcomes, the abuse of the National Guard Armies, the refusal to accept the legitimacy of elections, and the growing frequency and severity of threats of default and shutdowns, it is evident that the opposition party is clearing looking for alternative futures to pursue, and they actively practicing the tactics to achieve those goals. There is no other reason a current administration exposes the enlisted from an opposition party to the risks or death and dismemberment. Decisions have consequences, and because of the hyper-partisan and dangerous deployments of 2005 and 2009, there were several deaths and disabilities caused to the enlisted of states that should not have been there. Their sacrifice was not for the general welfare of the nation, but exclusively in preparation of the current administration to preserve power during a constitutional crisis. When one looks at the trend lines for the use of threats of default and government shutdowns, it is undeniable that as the number of threats increases, the likelihood of being acted on increases. Circumstances change, and a party unwilling to commit one year may be more willing to chance it the next year.

With the enhanced role national guard armies play in overseas deployments, there should be more scrutiny and regulation in the selection process for deployments. Many states have inalienable rights, like those guaranteed by the 2nd amendment (*of the U.S. Constitution*) to organize a well-regulated militia, and those of other sovereign powers established by the 10th amendment. To be clear, once the enlisted is isolated to a certain state, the unit falls under the authority of both the state and federal government as coequal operators. It is too dangerous to create an army exclusively from one state and then subject it to the partisan abuses of a hostile executive. A standing army is comprised of enlisted from all of the states, undifferentiated with no residency requirements, and should fall under the domain and exclusive authority of the federal government, but as soon as they are drawn from a single state, the authority is shared between the states. The possibility for abuse makes it imperative state governments gain more oversight and control over the deployment process, even if it is still subrogated to the federal government under certain situations. Even if not explicit declared in the Constitution, the federal government can provide the state executives the discretion to determine when their national guards are called for deployment. If they feel there is too much risk, in agreeing to the deployment, they have the authority to withhold them until it is safe to send their troops abroad or overseas. Legislatures have the authority and responsibility to regulate deployment procedures in order to protect the nation's war-readiness and trust in elections.

All national guard deployments processes should cease being secret process and become accessible for all state-level personnel to view along with the public. Any deployments, both abroad or domestic, must be split equally between the parties by numbers and type of enlisted deployed from each state. Projections must be made using current state executive party dispositions, and those for the next presidential election, so that a single deployment isn't compromised exclusively of one party for partisan reasons. Splitting the deployment by party is necessary to dispel any appearance of impropriety, making it much more likely state executives don't veto a deployment. A politically neutral deployment by design, will improve war-readiness by eliminating the risk of abuses.

When deployment schedules are being negotiated, they have to be approved by a bipartisan committee of state executives with approval by an armed services committee, where both the majority and minority parties are given the deployment schedules to consider. The public must be notified at least 6 months ahead of deployment, unless act of war declared by the federal legislature requires earlier deployments. State executives can object to national guard deployment at any time, electing to pay cumulative penalty to all federal tax subsidies received for every year access to the national guard is withheld from the federal government. The objecting is state automatically moved to the next years' deployment schedule. Penalties will remain in place for as long as there are scheduled National Guard deployments authorized by the legislature.

State are authorized to swap with other states so that the state executives can negotiate with other state executives for deployment. This flexibility will allow states to ensure they have proper coverage during Presidential transition years, and also negate the financial penalty for not allocating their guard to the current war-effort. Executives will generally authorize every deployment agreed to. Not only are the deployments public, discouraging abuses, but the states are incentivized to maintain veteran enlisted within their national guard armies. Veteran enlisted is the best way they can protect their residents civil rights and voting rights when threatened with enemies, both foreign and domestics. There would be significant blowback from voters if their enlisted were needlessly withheld, so the decision to withhold them will not be made lightly.

If an administration wants to veto the decision of the states' executive board, they can seek an injunction from federal judiciary, citing a national security justification, but it must be public verdict, and offer justification for not accepting the negotiated deployments agreed to by the states. This federal override exists in case there are no volunteer units, or every state withholds their units, forcing the federal government to make the selection, but constraints on political disposition of deployments still apply and are subject to review by the judiciary. Protections against an authoritarian abuse in the domestic theatre is more important than a short term disruption in national guard deployments, especially when a federal government has other mechanism, like a draft, to bolster the undifferentiated standing army that doesn't explicitly target the enlisted from a specific state.

Making national guard deployments a public display makes it impossible for a regime to make the units inaccessible to a state and then criminalizing the behavior of protest or criticizing the decision. Otherwise, an executive could send one party's national guard units to the border during an election or overseas to a war-zone, making the units inaccessible for a challenge to a compromised election, and subsequently arresting any sympathetic state executives or legislators if they protested the abuse. State executives still have the right to withhold their national guard units, but they will have to take their chances during the next election and pay a penalty on federalist tax dollars sent to the state. Giving the state executives a veto on the deployment of their national guards units, after involving them in the deployment negotiations, should eliminate must concerns national guard deployments can be weaponized during elections.

No nation is war-ready if they have doubts that one party will make dangerous and partisan deployments, denying other states access to their militias during compromised elections, or seeking to win elections by limiting death and disability of enlisted to those in opposition states. In order to regain war-readiness, a deployment process needs to be public with the proper checks and balances to ensure all states can defend themselves and their democratic entitlements. No nation is secure until their deployment process is both public and negotiated by the participants. The national guard is the front line defense against authoritarianism and a precipitous drop in the quality of democratic entitlements. All elected officials should respect those volunteering for their state militias and make every opportunity they aren't abused with unnecessary death and disability from partisan political deployments that also threaten the sovereignty of the states. One of the best indicators of character is how political parties treat their enlisted, or the enlisted from other states.

7 SYNTAX OF POWER

When a nation is threatened by authoritarianism, the biggest risk for democratic parties is the perpetually changing syntax of power. The constant churn of local, state, and federal elections results in unpredictable outcomes. A party may feel secure after a Presidential win in one cycle but a loss in the next could pose a clear and present danger. Majorities in the legislature rotate in and out after most election cycles forcing parties to make decision based on current conditions rather than future conditions. Timing is everything and although conflict is expected, the fog of war prevents parties from knowing which position they will occupy during an event.

Elections determine which party has higher ground during crises; it is much harder to defect from a democratic government than it is for democratic states to declare independence from an authoritarian regime. Every state represents millions of persons that may be left behind in authoritarian states with no civil rights and voting rights. When the risk of authoritarianism is present, every election could be the last election and inaction is just as consequential as mistaken action. If conflict looms on the horizon, the democratic party must choose when it takes place, even in circumstances where the odds of preserving the territorial integrity of the nation is low.

The democrats must provoke a conflict when they have the greatest chance to protect the greatest number of citizens. The alternative is risking everybody's safety with no chance of recovering voting rights and civil liberties. When democratic elections are suspended or compromised, there won't be any chance to use institutional protest to protect democracy. If the entire nation finds itself under the thrall of an authoritarian party, there won't be any chance for rescue. Democracy could be lost for generations.

Every weakness is exploited during a crisis. The worst should always be expected when your adversaries win nearly half of the seats in federal and state elections. After just one bad election cycle, authoritarians can force the democratic party into an inferior position, where retreating from the union is the only way they. There is no moral dilemma in secession. can still guarantee themselves access to free and fair elections. Separating themselves is also their best chance to protect those citizens left behind in an authoritarian nation. Free states can use economic sanctions and aid to coerce the authoritarian state into reform. Free states can lobby the international community to demand regime change. Free states present an opportunity to intervene with a military when other options fail. None of this is possible if the democratic party consents or collaborates with an authoritarian regime after a compromised election.

The democratic parties should not be overconfident when in power either, as due process can easily be bent towards the authoritarian party's interests. Debt defaults, government shutdowns, and tax protests can be lawfully deployed to win concessions from the democratic parties. Asymmetric warfare, utilizing institutional protests, can destabilize democratic regime making them more susceptible to secession or regime change. Democratic parties are expected to adhere to the law and all decisions rendered by the courts, making them more vulnerable to impeachments, stoppages in appropriations, and disruptions in credit. There is always the risk next election appoints a despot, bringing the threat for peaceful transition to an authoritarian administration, which subsequently relies on anti-democratic policies to subvert future elections.

Elections determine position the parties are in during a conflict, and position dictates outcomes. In order for an opposition party to secede, they will need almost unanimous consent from their institutions. The opposition party will need to occupy the governor's office with majorities in the state legislature. Without these homogenous political outcomes, they won't be able to pass laws declaring their independence, nor will they be able to fund the war effort and coordinate with other seceding states. In order to implement policy, they must first pass the law through the legislature, and then enforce the law through the executive branch. Without support from both of these branches of government, opposition leaders are unlikely pursue their constituent's interests.

Requiring unanimous consent of institutions is a natural failsafe protecting democracies against secession, but when an authoritarian is in power, it makes it far less likely the democrats are able to organize themselves into a formal resistance. Not only will confidence and courage be in short supply, but the numbers of core states with control over both the executive and legislative branches will be few in number. Most of the states will have mixed electoral outcomes, implicitly strengthening the federal government's position. These periphery states won't be able to contribute significant capital, supplies, or enlisted to the resistance movement, unless consented to by both establishment and opposition parties.

The United States is a great case study in how postponing a conflict can result in millions of persons losing their freedoms after just one bad election cycle. If an authoritarian party was to win the Presidential election, and homogenous political power on the state level is needed for the states to separate themselves, it would result in tens of millions of citizens losing access to voting rights in states with mixed electoral outcomes. For example, if the democratic party was in an inferior position, in 2020, 4.6 million residents in Louisiana[106], 10.5 million residents in North Carolina[107], and 7.3 million in Kansas and Kentucky[108], might be locked

---

[106] U.S. Census Bureau, "State Population Totals and Components of Change: 2010-2019", U.S. Census Bureau, accessed on Aug 14, 2020, retrieved from
  https://www2.census.gov/pro-gramssurveys/popest/data-sets/2010-2019/national/totals/nst-est2019-alldata.csv?#
[107] U.S. Census Bureau, "State Population Totals and Components of Change: 2010-2019", U.S. Census Bureau, accessed on Aug 14, 2020, retrieved from
  https://www2.census.gov/pro-gramssurveys/popest/data-sets/2010-2019/national/totals/nst-est2019-alldata.csv?#

into an authoritarian union by heterogenous electoral outcomes. There is no way a state with a Democratic governor acquires the majorities in the Republican state legislature needed to secede from the union. The Midwest won't fare much better than the South. Wisconsin and Michigan represent another 16 million who likely lack the homogenous political outcome to secede from an authoritarian regime or support the democrats resisting them[109]. Even Pennsylvania and Minnesota, with a combined population of 18.4 million residents, suffer mixed electoral outcomes and may be forced to remain in an authoritarian union[110]. Democracy is decided on the margins of elections, and one election cycle could mean the difference between democracy or authoritarianism for nearly 57 million people.

In 2020, 20 Republican states have control over the legislature and Governor's office while only 7 Democratic states are uniform in control. Parties controlling both the governor's office and legislature are considered to have trifectas. The current number of trifecta states in the United States demonstrates the significant obstacles not occupying the Oval Office is during a contested election or civil war. When the Democrats are in the Oval Office, they can rely on the support of all states with mixed outcomes, resulting in 30 states continuing to contribute enlisted and tax revenues. Republicans will only have access to 20 states for enlisted and revenues when they normally have the support of 30. Nearly a third of predictably Republican states won't be able to secede or support the insurrection. The location of the 10 could present more problems for supply chains and troop

---

[108] U.S. Census Bureau, "State Population Totals and Components of Change: 2010-2019", U.S. Census Bureau, accessed on Aug 14, 2020, retrieved from
  https://www2.census.gov/pro-gramssurveys/popest/data-sets/2010-2019/national/totals/nst-est2019-alldata.csv?#
[109] U.S. Census Bureau, "State Population Totals and Components of Change: 2010-2019", U.S. Census Bureau, accessed on Aug 14, 2020, retrieved from
  https://www2.census.gov/pro-gramssurveys/popest/data-sets/2010-2019/national/totals/nst-est2019-alldata.csv?#
[110] U.S. Census Bureau, "State Population Totals and Components of Change: 2010-2019", U.S. Census Bureau, accessed on Aug 14, 2020, retrieved from
  https://www2.census.gov/pro-gramssurveys/popest/data-sets/2010-2019/national/totals/nst-est2019-alldata.csv?#

movements for the confederacy. However. if the federal government is humbled by debt defaults and government shutdowns, the advantages go back to the Republican states who control more governors and trifecta governments. The Democrats will only be able to rely on their core 7 states for revenues and enlisted. States with only Governors can provide only limited support, until new appropriations are needed.

The low probability of the Democrats successfully protecting the nation even when in the Oval Office increases the risk of authoritarianism when they are out of office. If the Republicans use a debt default and government shutdown to disable the federal government, they could quickly overwhelm the uncoordinated and confused Democratic states. Not only is secession likely, but the Democrats are likely to end up occupied by the Republican confederacy, despite occupying the Oval Office. The odds get much worse of the Republicans are in the Oval Office and refuse to leave after a compromised election or some other event preserving their incumbent position. If the Republicans refuse to vacate the office, the Democrats can't rely on the state governments to remove them. They fully depend on tradition and due process for a peaceful transition. If anything were to interrupt this process; they will more than likely be unable to protest the acts or successfully secede, setting up every incentive for the Republicans to resist peaceful regime change. With most of the incentives rewarding bad behavior, and with all of the demographic changes and economic conditions pointing towards future election losses for Republicans, it makes sense to act on their instinct now when favorable outcomes are more predictable.

The Democrats are better off provoking a conflict while in Oval Office because it optimizes their outcomes. There is a known risk of conflict in an environment of debt default threats, government shutdowns, and compromised elections, and the Democrats can eliminate or mitigate the worst outcomes by choosing when to engage the Republicans. The odds aren't great for Democrats to preserve the nation from either position, but the likelihood of remaining free in more states is much higher when occupying the federal executive branch. The Democrats have to weigh all possible outcomes, not just ideal outcomes, and choose the strategy that maximizes utility from an average of outcomes if they can't completely control all inputs. A Nash Equilibrium points towards conflict; if 3 of the 4 highest point outcomes result in a split up of the United States, both parties have to prepare for conflict.

If the only quadrant that both preserves the territorial boundaries of the nation and democratic process, has the least point value for the opposition party, and also occurs on the same side of an outcome resulting in authoritarianism, then the administration must see the optimal outcome as least likely and also contributing to the worst outcomes. When incentives are reciprocal and exclusionary, both parties will have to take adversarial positions when negotiating through position and timing. The ideal outcome produces the worst possible outcome when only one player takes an adversarial position. The presence of debt defaults, government shutdowns, and compromised elections clearly indicates a one party already assuming an adversarial position making it the most dangerous strategy to pursue.

Political parties have a responsibility to maximize utility for the largest number of constituents, even if this is a suboptimal result when compared to the ideal outcome. Game theory is a useful tool for analyzing incentives to assess the probability of an event occurring. It also is a useful implement for evaluating all possibly outcomes. Looking at the average outcome for a series of potential outcomes is a more effective strategy as people and parties often pursue the most accessible outcomes in a dynamic environment that changes resulting from prior outputs. Looking at the average amount, accommodates a larger number of associated outcomes when there are information asymmetries and newly acquired known inputs.

If the next executive election brings with it a heightened the risk of authoritarianism, the current incumbent has the responsibility to provoke an incident while still in office. It shouldn't be hard when budgets are negotiated with threats of default and government shutdowns. Every law enforcement officer knows it is better to provoke a perpetrator while they are aware of their circumstances then to disengage and let the criminal provoke conflict on their terms. If the opposition relents and makes concessions, it is a better indicator that they won't try to usurp power while in office or secede when the opportunity presents itself. The opposition party is pursuing authoritarianism, they are more likely to strike out in anger and prematurely secede. Even if this results in suboptimal outcomes, it avoids the worst possible outcomes which were more demonstrated to be more likely than initially suspected. If the opposition party starts making concessions while out of office, they are more likely to accept concessions while in office. If no concessions are being made, the establishment party immediately assume the worst possible outcomes if they vacate the executive branch and the other party has a history of resisting peaceful regime changes.

If the Democrats can provoke the Republicans into seceding prior to defaulting on the federal government's debt or shutting it down. Without a debt default or government shutdown, the Democrats can depend on 30 states for enlisted and revenues, more or less. If there is a default or shutdown, the number of reliable states drops down to just 7. The dramatic effects of institutional protests are known to both parties, and is evidenced by their near ubiquitous use whenever a Democratic president is in office. In fact, they are only generally employed when the Republicans are out of office, which contributes to a culture of concessions and collaboration within the Democratic Party. It is a Hobson's choice between losing half the states to secession or losing them all to authoritarianism, especially when Democrats don't rely on institutional protests to coerce their own reforms from the establishment party. Economic conditions will continue to deteriorate while the public has less and less trust in elections, and their outcomes, until most of the public support some form or radical action.

In ideal circumstance for loyalists, dissidents will remain disorganized and noncommittal. If the odds of successful secession are small, the chances they risk their lives is smaller. One aspect is in direct proportion to the other. If the federal government maintains borrowing authority, appropriations authority, and access to law enforcement agencies to investigate and apprehend the dissidents, the cost of rebellion becomes too great. There is an inverse relationship here; the longer the insurrection takes to form, the lower the probability of victory. Individuals can be arrested, and states can be discouraged by public policy and criminal sanctions. If the secessionists hesitate, their discovery may impact elections, effectively removing them from office and ending the threat.

If the rebel states lose their inhibitions and strike out in anger by prematurely declaring secession, they will no longer be able to vote on internal matters for the nation. When they withdraw their representatives, it is far less likely those representatives that remain will be able to impose government shutdowns and debt defaults, or pursuing impeachment. If the federal government maintains borrowing and appropriations authority, they are much more likely to win the war. After the states declare an intent to secede, the federal government can pursue treason charges and arrest the leadership. A declaration of secession is the most counter-productive decision a group of states can make before a conflict.

Only those states that have governors and majorities in the legislature from the same party will have the opportunity to ratify a secession with the authority of the law. This should be a smaller number than the total number of states that support secession. It will be these core states that provide most of the funding for the confederacy. They can lawfully raise revenues for armies and divert revenues away from the union. The states can openly resist federal law enforcement operating within their jurisdictions, and they can reach out to former adversaries and allies in hopes of finding support for their new state. More importantly, if these first states successfully secede, they will provide a model for other states to leave the union. Other governors stand a better chance of ratifying secession, if they can immediately join an alternative union. The federal government will need to act swiftly, with determination and certainty, if it is to retain its territorial integrity.

Uncommitted states, remaining in the union but on the periphery, will create a fugue of uncertainty and resist all efforts to intervene. A crisis in leadership is one of the biggest risks facing both sides of a secession when a government shutdown is imposed. The establishment states may have elected a president, but that president will not be able to deploy law enforcement and military assets without appropriation powers. The president will be mostly ceremonial during the shutdown, which is contradictory to their expectations, presenting a greater chance for conflict within the establishment party. All of the available cash flows and tax revenues will be diverted back to the core states who have appropriation authority but no central direction. When the president can only offer advice on how the troops are used, the governors can disregard it and follow their own intuitions and analysis. Without a cohesive leader with a central intelligence source, the governors won't be able to coordinate their forces in the fog of war.

There is a more eloquent solution that contracting out federal assets to a decentralized armed force. The loyalist states could incorporate a temporary union to redirect the state revenues back to the elected president, outside the confines of the shutdown, in order to preserve the leadership of the union and more effectively coordinate the states. This temporary union would accept the results of the former election but exclude the periphery states who may still tentatively support the secessionists, eliminating any risk to future borrowing authority and appropriations authority. The states can ratify the incorporation and fully fund it, after military assets and law enforcements assets are transferred.

States that have governors and legislative majorities are the core states that can pass laws creating a new union that imports the former unions federal laws and representational systems. The core states can pass appropriation bills and maintain legitimate standing armies while the former union is mired in a government shutdown or where a legislature can't get a quorum to pass laws dealing with the secession. These states can still coordinate with periphery states that may only have governors in office who can contribute more limited resources through executive power rather than legislative powers. Working together, the combined forces should be able to mount a considerable defense of the nation, while abiding by all of the constitutional conditions of the original union.

A clause in the temporary union will require it to disincorporate when the threat ends. Another clause will require a constitutional convention to decide on new representational systems if the schism proves to be permanent. This allows states to quickly assemble an emergency union during a time of crisis, deleverage it after the threat ends, or move forward with forming a new durable government if the separation is permanent. Leaving zero probability for internal conflict or disagreement during the crisis is the best way to guarantee success. It will also attract more support from the periphery states or those wavering between independence and loyalty. With more certainty around the concept of an emergency union, there will be less resistance to joining the government, and absolutely no questions about when it should be disbanded or canonized.

The last clause in the emergency declaration deals with the new union assuming the prior obligations of the former union. Establishing credit after a default or secession is one of the most pressing issues facing the nation. Without borrowing, it is very unlikely the nation can raise the cash needed to prosecute the war while still providing government services. Assuming liability for the former treasuries will restore faith in the credit of the protesting states. However, the states can choose which creditors are paid and by what rate, ensuring the new temporary union isn't inundated with the former nation's debt during the crisis. They may take on a large amount of debt, but they will also have more predictable access to future cash revenues from borrowing.

Bills authorizing these incorporations can be written in preparation of the emergency and only passed or implemented during a crisis. States can pen these laws and shelve them until they are needed, updating them every budget cycle as part of an emergency preparation plan for government continuity during a disaster. Current emergency management agencies consider hurricanes, earthquakes, fires, and terrorist attacks. It is not a heavy lift to consider debt defaults and government shutdowns similar threats with detailed plans for emergency intervention. Preparation permits a speedy response, increasing the odds of preserving the territorial boundaries of the union. A faster and stronger response should also discourage more states from commit to the secession.

State governments must also demonstrate initiative and scrutinize their supply chains for equipment during emergencies. If parts for durable products come from other states, it may make it impossible to assemble or purchase the products, rendering the Air forces, Navy, or other units dependent on airplanes, boats, and heavy vehicles less effective during a prolonged conflict. Even if they have current inventory, replacement parts and repairs will become less and less available. There could be natural barriers, trade barriers, or other disruptions to the supply chain, placing significant emphasis on the national guard armies which can be housed and supplied on a local level. They will be able to operate more effectively with locally resourced small arms and communications equipment.

The states must study their finances in the context of a debt default or prolonged government shutdown. If there is a debt default, states will want to prepare emergency policies to respond to disrupted bond markets or economies in recession. The states will want a clear picture of which federal liabilities that can be assumed and how their agencies are impacted by losses of subsidies. When the federal government is compromised, it shifts priority to the state and city governments, which must be in a position to leverage their balance sheets and personnel.

If the states do not prepare emergency policies before an institutional protest, the only other way a union can prevent states from seceding is relying on authoritarian executive policies to bypass legislative obstruction or government shutdowns. This brings more risk to the union. If the establishment states rely on authoritarian policies to prevent secession, it will provoke more peripheral states to defect to the resistance movement or justifying states remaining on the sidelines. Any change in the support for the protesting states could extend the length of the conflict, inviting more opportunities for impeachment, default, or local and state elections, changing the calculus for winning the war.

The United States also presents a study in how establishment governments benefit from leveraging a fully funded federal government. The original invasion force in Iraq required 161,000 soldiers to subdue a nation of about 25 million persons[111]. The combined population of the Northeast, Midwest, and West Coast is roughly 6.6 times greater than Iraq, requiring an estimated 1,062,000 soldiers. This threshold is nearly met by the current standing army. Even after National Guard and Reserve forces from the opposition party are deducted, the United States has more than 837,000 enlisted with about 132,000 federal law enforcement officers available to aid in the occupation, bringing the total number of forces available to 969,000 for the establishment government. When Air Force and Marines are tallied it carries the number well beyond the threshold of the 1,062,000 troops needed to successfully occupy a population of 165 million persons.

The federal government will have more than 4:1 advantage in enlisted unless the opposition party relies on institutional protests to even the odds. Prolonged government shutdowns will produce high rates of defection in enlisted military and law enforcement agencies after the federal government stops paying them. State Unemployment benefits will only last 6 months without new authorizations from the legislature. Most federal personnel will not be able to remain unemployed for much longer if they have mortgages to pay and families to care for. Many enlisted will opt to go home and join their state's National Guard unit or law enforcement agency rather than the federal military organizing to occupy their community. Protesting states benefit twice from defections: every person who joins the state militia reduces the total number of establishment forces, making it doubly as effective as new recruits.

Demographics may play a significant role in defections, when the states with the largest representation in the military are also the states with the largest minority concentrations in the union[112]. Although officers in the U.S. military remain nearly 80% Caucasian, enlisted numbers demonstrate a considerable increase in minority enlistment from prior years[113].

---

[111] Amy Belasco, "Troop Levels in the Afghan and Iraq Wars, FY2001-FY2012: Cost and Other Potential Issues", Congressional Research Service, July 2, 2009, retrieved from https://fas.org/sgp/crs/natsec/R40682.pdf.
[112] CFR.org Editors, "Demographics of the U.S. Military", Council on Foreign Relations, Updated July 13th, 2020, retrieved from https://www.cfr.org/backgrounder/demographics-us-military

In 2004, the composition was 36% minority and 64% Caucasian, and in 2020, 43% of enlisted are minority and only 57% are Caucasian[114]. With nearly 80% of the commissioned officers being Caucasian, but only 57% of the enlisted, it is critical for an opposition party to shut down the government to promote defection from the standing military. Otherwise, the 43% of the enlisted who don't identify as Caucasian, will likely maintain a regimented hierarchy under the command of the establishment party. By shutting down the government and ending enlisted pay, the opposition party can better guarantee more of the assets leave the federal military and join the state militaries.

The democratic states will benefit from retaining 100% loyalty in their own National Guard units where the states with large minority populations could see defection rates of 20-30% for regular enlisted, seriously eroding the reliability of federal enlisted during a crisis. The democratic states need only draw away 25%, or 1/3rd of the remaining troops, to their side in order to equal the total number of federal enlisted. The odds improve when democratic states add 500,000 police personnel to the tally of assets. Even without any violence, the implied threat of losing support nearly half their enlisted should be enough for authoritarian governments to make the necessary concession to presence both peace and democracy.

The democratic party's best strategy is to rely on lawful and nonviolent institutional protests to neutralize a federal executive branch while the parties negotiate an end to the hostilities. The longer outright violence is delayed, the better the chances for the democratic states to remain free and unoccupied. The average annual cost of the Iraq War was $100.2B from 2003 through 2011[115]. If the population of the

---

[113] CFR.org Editors, "Demographics of the U.S. Military", Council on Foreign Relations, Updated July 13th, 2020, retrieved from
https://www.cfr.org/backgrounder/demographics-us-military
[114] Amanda Barroso, "The changing profile of the U.S. military: Smaller in size, more diverse, more women in leadership", Pew Research Center, Sep 10, 2019, retrieved from https://www.pewresearch.org/fact-tank/2019/09/10/the-changing-profile-of-the-u-s-military/
[115] Kimberly Amadeo, "Cost of Iraq War, Its Timeline, and the Economic Impact", The Balance, Updated July 15, 2020, retrieved from
https://www.thebalance.com/cost-of-iraq-war-timeline-economic-impact-

democratic states is 6.6 times as large as Iraq, the war effort to occupy them could cost nearly $680B a year. When the democratic states implement tax protests, the establishment party's entire discretion sector budget amounts to just $560B, with a $335B peace-time defense budget[116].

If an additional $680B is needed to wage war, the extra borrowing represents nearly 121% of the Republican states total discretionary budget. Every year this deficit spending is authorized, it will add nearly 7.3% to the debt: GDP ratio of a $9.2T dollar economy. In just 4 years the federal government accumulates 30% of GDP in debt even before any stimulus to the economy is considered. The federal government will have to raise taxes considerably to continue the war effort, creating an inflationary cycle that leads to less economic output, lower government revenues, and a stronger economic correction after the shutdown, default, and tax protests.

In worst-case scenarios, the budget for the year would have already passed, giving the federal government temporary access to revenues they can move around for emergency spending. As soon as the government shutdown starts, the clock starts. Protesting states may only need to defend themselves with their national guard and police for just over a year. Emergency funding will eventual dry up and without subsequent acts from Congress subsidizing an illegal war of occupation, the military would run out of munitions, durable products, and could make payroll. Sure, the federal government has a military nearly four times as large, but it might not have the authority to deploy them, or the credit needed to fund them for much longer than a few months.

Numbers don't lie. When the opposition can deploy institutional protests prior to an armed conflict, they immediately even the odds of coercing reform or regime change, by avoiding the violence or overcoming it. If one looks at the enlistment figures for the United States, it is apparent that position means everything when democracies go to war with themselves. This is why institutional protests like debt defaults, government shutdowns, and tax protests are so

---

3306301.

[116] The states were divided between parties in the same allocation present on pp 44-45.

important. Not only can they result in peaceful regime change but they can eliminate the institutional advantages earned by the federal government if violent conflict ensues. The opposition party can withhold appropriations, ending the threat of occupation by federal law enforcement and military assets. When the establishment party oversteps their constitutional authority trying to overcome these obstacles, the opposition party can impeach the president.

Even suboptimal outcome requires tremendous work by those trying to defend their political rights. Any party that thinks they have an innate advantage will be proved wrong, when they don't acquire the homogenous political outcomes needed to protest, or they lose their borrowing and appropriations authorities needed to preserve the territorial boundaries. The party that practices the rhetoric of institutional protests and pursues anti-democratic strategies is far more likely to come out on top. Poor outcomes are even more likely when democratic parties enforce competitive elections that give an authoritarian party more opportunities to win in their districts while anti-democratic laws in other states prevent reciprocity. When political parties bend the rules and cheat, they are more likely to find themselves in a superior position, and position means everything before a predictable conflict. The syntax of power can be ruthlessly unforgiving, especially if the political parties aren't open about the actual conditions facing the nation. Unless the public has an opportunity to price in their preferences and expectations for elections, there will only be disappointment and surprise when the wrong party is in office during an event.

Many nations that have had civil wars in the past, pass laws mitigating the chances of future rebellions in the future. For example, the United States passed the 14th amendment which allows Congress to expel or refuse to seat Representatives supporting secession or rebellion. This reduces the effectiveness of using government shutdowns, but does not entirely mitigate the strategy. The 14th amendment offers absolutely no protections against a debt default, which will have already occurred before the 14th amendment can used. The Congress may have to hold long court hearings, with appellate and supreme courts weighing in order to expel them. This takes time which the nation doesn't have with a debt default. Even a government shutdown is still modestly effective, if they can keep the government shutdown for a few months while the state governments organize and mobile. Even then, representatives are exercising their lawful powers to appropriate and pass laws, so there may be significant support for their behavior in the court systems. There is no intrinsic difference between a party threaten default to reduce the deficit and one considering secession or dissolution. The courts may not be able to intervene effectively when the Constitution offers contradictory powers and amendments. Whenever discretion is involved, the outcomes remain unknown and risk is pervasive.

When representatives are removed from office, it gives the governors and states another opportunity to install senators or representatives that support debt defaults and government shutdowns. The federal executive has no power to remove governors, and the governors can repeatedly appoint representatives that will pursue shutdowns and defaults. It will be a messy process, prosecuted over several months or years, with many opportunities for the rebel states to evolve their strategies and improve their odds of winning a war of succession or a war of secession. Once an administration acts to arrest senators, representatives, or governors the states will have justification for secession, when they effectively lose representation in the union. Although the states will lose access to the federal government's finances and elections, they may still be formidable adversaries. Enlisted may still defect. The states already have access to National Guard armies and a number of veteran police officers that rival the number of current enlisted. Tax protests can still defund the federal government, resulting in other threats of default or government shutdown. Expelling senators and representatives will only harden the rebel states and possibly bolster support by the public. The public is likely to interpret the excising of representatives as authoritarianism and antidemocratic, especially if the establishment party is trying to control legislative outcomes.

When the federal government arrests political operatives, it gives the power the court system. Not only could prosecutors and judges intervene unfavorably, but juries may resist the charges. This introduces a series of known unknowns that will impact future elections. If there is any weakness in the cases or arguments, the rebel party members could be emboldened by the lack of prosecution. The outcome of future elections is even more uncertain if the public sees the expulsions as antidemocratic or authoritarian. The risk is significant, especially if the rebel party remains disciplined and uncommunicative in their ultimate agenda. If they don't openly declare their intent to secede, then they are exercising their Constitutional powers and are less likely to be successfully prosecuted. Not only could this impact future elections, increasing the risk of authoritarianism, but the courts may intervene on the side of the rebel parties, reinforcing their access to threats of debt defaults and government shutdowns. Judges are appointed and often can't be removed, unlike senators and representatives, making it a more durable and imminent risk. The nation could be in for the fight of its life, where a future election could result in occupation just as easily as losing a martial contest, or a judicial ruling could result in the ruin of the nation's public finance, punctuating the end of a political union with a dissolution.

Laws like the 14th amendment can reduces the odds a minority party organized a revolt. It may even mitigate the effectiveness of some of the tools, but it can't completely inoculate the nation against future rebellions. Government shutdowns and debt defaults are lawful exercises which makes them more dangerous than other behaviors. Whenever they are present in the political discourse of a nation, the parties should be wary of an opposition party organizing towards revolution. Calculating the odds of successfully defending the nation will have to accommodate the state and federal court systems, in addition to state and federal legislature elections, and state and federal executive election, putting it well beyond the reach of any quick speculation or modest research. The vectors will be rapidly changing if senators and representatives are arrested, a congress refuses to unseat political opponents, or tax protests defund the federal government to the point a where war isn't a viable option. The syntax of power is incredibly important but it can only assist in prediction when the dynamic calculus changes as politics operatives take action, the courts render decisions, and the public mobilize in protest or open rebellion.

9 OUTSIDE INFLUENCE

Institutional protests like debt defaults, government shutdowns, and tax protests are the most effective way to coerce regime change peaceably. It is also the most effective way to complement armed resistance when open rebellion is the only recourse left to an exploited and oppressed people. Without appropriations authority and borrowing authority, an executive will be unable to lawfully intervene in a military buildup on the state-level. After the violent conflict starts, an institutional protest can cripple the finances of a federal government giving the rebels or secessionists their best opportunity to succeed.

This process can be refined and tailored to specific constitutions found in the world, providing reproducible and effective strategies for regime change, rebellion, or secession in democratic nations that are targeted. Nearly 55% of are rated as flawed or hybrid and thus susceptible to intervention[117]. Intelligence agencies must adapt to the new environment and adopt policies and procedures that leverage due process in influence and aid campaigns.

There is only one benefit to the increase in frequency and severity of public finance crises in the United States. The reoccurring insults provides a template for coercing regime change in other failing or lower-quality democracies. It is a model for democratic parties and their allies to use when retaliating against authoritarian parties starting to consolidate power around illegitimate elections or anti-democratic policies. It is much more effective for a democratic party to

---

[117] Economist Intelligence Unit, "Democracy Index 2019: A year of democratic setbacks and popular protest", The Economist, Accessed Aug 6, 2020, retrieved from http://www.eiu.com/Handlers/WhitepaperHandler.ashx?fi=Democracy-Index-2019.pdf&mode=wp&campaignid=democracyindex-2019, pp 3.

intervene before they lose their political power, rather than from a minority party position with no expectation of honest or accurate elections, and no access to recourse through institutional protests.

Without clear instructions and leadership, many parties will hesitate. Urgency will paralyze them with fear and a lack of preparation fills them with doubt. Making an error in application of a debt default or permanent shutdown is terrifying; a misapplied institutional protest could establish precedent for authoritarian polices arresting politicians or suppressing protestors. These risks can be mitigated when institutional protests are studied beforehand. The chances of a mistake are far less when the policies are rehearsed. The political parties will have more confidence opposing authoritarians when they all make the same observations and come to the same conclusions. Institutional protests are easily reproducible in most presidential democracies, especially when they are contemplated ahead of time and comported to the due process of specific nations.

When democratic parties can identify authoritarian threats ahead of time, they can start developing contingency plans and inculcating their constituents to the rhetoric of government shutdowns and threats of default. If institutional protests had been more accessible to the democratic parties in Hungary and Poland, these nations may have fended off the authoritarians currently in power. If the democratic parties were aggressively pursuing government shutdowns with tax protests and debt defaults, the authoritarians may have retreated. At the very least, the democratic parties would have been in a far stronger position to defend themselves through military force if the authoritarians did not relent.

When conflict is inevitable, institutional protests will be the most effective nonviolent and consequential method to achieve reform or regime change. The arguments for institutional protests can come out of universities, think tanks, and elected officials. Persons with well-established academic credentials can proffer support for debt defaults and government shutdowns without raising any suspicion. Civil society and due process are built on a foundation of free speech, rights to organize, protest, and debate. These policies can be freely practiced by elected representatives, giving them inscrutable legitimacy. Often, the culture will already be steeped in the prior episodes of debt defaults and government shutdowns and be highly receptive of the continued use of institutional protests. The risks will be well known and the consequences will be understood.

Larger nations are more susceptible to the organic growth of fundamentalism simply due to the specialization of labor and the great diversity in experiences and preferences of its citizens. In a natural experiment, foreign nations will be able to examine which ideas have traction and apply leverage when they feel it is in their best interests. The source for funding and promoting these ideas can be obfuscated through private contracts and business networks. A foreign nation could easily funnel money to a think tank that already specializes in the rhetoric, making many of the academics and researchers unwitting participants. In the United States, "Colleges universities failed to disclose more than $6.5 billion in funding from foreign countries, including China, Russia, Saudi Arabia, the United Arab Emirates and Qatar"[118]. This intersection of foreign interests with domestic interests won't immediately be recognizable as a threat; private industry and institutional are free to research and advocate for almost any policy they can rationalize.

The ideas fomented by the private industry can be acted upon during periods of social unrest or political turmoil. All of the work will be accomplished during peacetime or the lead up to an event. When the crisis starts, foreign money can flood into the country, helping to organize local protest groups, shape the blogosphere, or influence social media. Word of mouth and social media presents an imminent threat when the policies have made it into mainstream politics. In the political arena the ideas can be perfected, the arguments supporting them can be sharpened, and future electoral performance estimated. When institutional protests are openly debated or advocated within the legislature, they are much more likely to

---

[118] Lauren Camera, "Billion in Foreign Aid to Colleges and Universities Goes Undetected", U.S. News, Oct. 20, 2020, retrieved from
https://www.usnews.com/news/education-news/articles/2020-10-20/billions-in-foreign-aid-to-colleges-and-universities-goes-undetected

be acted on during a crisis. Regime change requires foresight and planning, but when a crisis emerges, it will help the opposition party to seize the opportunity

Prior to the climax of a constitutional crisis, foreign involvement may be been indistinguishable from any of the acts and beliefs of ordinary citizens and domestic institutions. The more stress there is within the nation, the less scrutiny there will be on outside influence from within these groups and institutions. Foreign agents can stir up support for the institutional protests as a means to add accelerant to an already explosive situation. Nations permitting private campaign finance and other acts of official corruption are the most susceptible to these strategies. When speakers comingle financial interests with principles, the miasma of corruption and compromise will bend the culture towards deregulated industries, defunded governments, and sectarian divisions within the public.

One example of such an arrangement in the United States is the American Legislative Exchange Council (ALEC). ALEC is an organization composed of lobbyists and supported by companies that researches and writes conservatives laws and distributes them to city, state, and federal lawmakers as templates that can easily pass when majorities are earned. Groups like ALEC give political parties the tools they need to organize dangerous anti-tax movements, small arms proliferation, and the austerity measures needed to undermine a democratic government. In the United States, ALEC has contributed to an era of unprecedented deregulation and underfunded governments.

Other nations may be just as vulnerable as the United States to anti-tax and weak regulatory policies that make a nation susceptible to regime change. The incentives found in capitalist economy and democracy result in a naive susceptibility to corruption and exploitation. The rhetoric is already common among conservative groups and politicians, and with just a little prodding, an environment of perpetual debt defaults and government shutdowns can be cultivated.

ALEC is a lawful organization that merely pursues its stakeholders' interests, making groups like it an incredible tool for Intelligence Agencies intending to influence wavering democracies. When a nation is identified as corrupt, illiberal, or inefficient, it can be infiltrated by intelligence operatives that openly promote destabilizing policies and institutional protests. The public will be more likely to support with foreign policy that enables an opposition party to peaceable coerce regime change with protests supported by government shutdowns. The intervention has to be timed well and practiced before the democratic party vacates too many seats and loses the ability to act on other institutional protests, but the threat of authoritarianism invites the culture of institutional protests into ordinary political discourse.

Intelligence agencies have another reason to pursue and promote institutional protests. Peaceful and non-violent strategies should be more cost effective and less risky than war for regime change. It is easier and cheaper to assemble a team of lawyers to assess the due process of a target nation and then write laws for lobbyists, than to covertly intervene with violence. Most of this labor can be conducted long before there is any commitment for intervention. The laws can be researched and written years before an event, and only updated when necessary. Nearly half of the world's governments are democratic and flawed democracies are the most susceptible to nonviolent interventions based on protests and due process. Intelligence agencies will want to adapt to the new strategies, if those strategies can be tested first and develop histories that demonstrate proven success[119].

Intelligence agencies should have departments set aside to contract out with lobbyists, lawyers, and former representatives of a host country targeted for regime change. There, the contractors can examine the pathways towards an institutional protest like a default or government shutdown. The departments can examine all of the ways due process can be used to coerce regime change and remove an authoritarian during a crisis. They can ready laws to be passed on the state level, to enforce tax protests and set up the financial, legal,

---

[119] Economist Intelligence Unit, "Democracy Index 2019: A year of democratic setbacks and popular protest", The Economist, Accessed Aug 6, 2020, retrieved from http://www.eiu.com/Handlers/WhitepaperHandler.as-hx?fi=Democracy-Index-2019.pdf&mode=wp&campaignid=democracyindex-2019, pp 3.

and operations infrastructure to engage in resistance. The opposition can act quickly, with due process and authority on their side. It may be their best and only chance to dislodge an authoritarian from power before that person consolidates their position and makes peaceful resolutions unattainable.

The resistance will need to be highly capitalized and partnered with law firms to initiate a ground swell of private and public lawsuits on every misappropriation or overstep during the government shutdowns. It helps to predict which arguments are legitimate and effective before starting a shutdown, so that the party can efficiently allocate labor and capital resources to the productive lawsuits. Most nations have highly visible constitutions and legal cannons available for research. Time is on the side of the party that carefully plans a response, rather than haphazardly falling into a crisis, after disregarding the signs of conflict.

The use of institutional protests should completely nullify any advantage an establishment party has when wielding federal government as a tool for oppression. With no appropriations powers, no revenues, and no credit, the federal government will have to meet the demands of the opposition party and public. If they don't, they will have to rely on state revenues to support federal agencies suffering under significant defection rates in enlisted and federal personnel. There is plenty of time between when an institutional protest starts, and when it may end in violence, and at any point the establishment party can make the necessary concessions and compromises to satisfy the demands of the public. When institutional protests are used, the 53% rate of success for peaceful protests should increase considerably, along with the 26% success rate for violent movements.

Nearly 75% of the world's countries have at least some democratic institutions or voting rights, and many of these nations are steeped in corruption, inefficiency, and wealth inequality[120]. The environment is ripe for opposition parties to

---

[120] Economist Intelligence Unit, "Democracy Index 2019: A year of democratic setbacks and popular protest", The Economist, Accessed Aug 6, 2020, retrieved from http://www.eiu.com/Handlers/WhitepaperHandler.as-hx?fi=Democracy-Index-2019.pdf&mode=wp&campaignid=democracyindex-2019, pp 3.

peaceably coerce regime change, demand reforms, or pursue outright coups using institutional protests. If the nations don't already have laws on the books that support lawful institutional protest, opposition parties are likely to pursue laws that make future challenges more successful. It might take years or decades, but the architecture for institutional protests can be slowly built up, in expectation of possible conflict.

Preparing institutional protests requires hours of professional labor but this strategy is still more cost effective than conventional warfare. Everything can be prepared ahead of time, offline, and updated only periodically. If the estimates and assumptions are accurate, the opposition party will immediately recognize the threat and start searching out for information that could aid them. Step by step plans for introducing legislation or imposing an institutional protest will be discreetly communicated through academic and private channels before a more formal resistance is mobilized against the encroaching authoritarian. Democracies would no longer have to sit idly by and watch allies decline into totalitarianism.

The first step is to outline the proper procedure for imposing an institutional protest like a prolonged government shutdown or tax protest. They need to note which chambers can provoke the shutdown. They also need to answer which chambers can prolong it. The political parties should be researching prior episodes to see how morally flexible their constituents are when supporting new threats of default or prolonged shutdown. Analytical politics is a science that enables limited predictions, and political parties or outside agencies will want to know the exact parameters for support or success before they act on the emergency measures. The agents will need to know precisely when to act and when to relent. This calls for established guidelines with evidence to support the conclusions.

There is an order to effective government shutdowns. The opposition party must have enough electoral wins to remain in office and enforce the shutdown. This is the only way they can peaceably coerce regime change or reform from the authoritarian party. They can't succumb to their animal instincts and declare independence too early. Instead, they must pursue every legitimate means for reform and regime change before joining in open rebellion of an authoritarian administration. They must remember to stay in office, to preserve a quorum (or block one), in order to prevent the authoritarian government from resuming regular appropriations and borrowing. They have to be discreet when they start bulking up state military and police assets while the federal government is restrained. In order to maximize their chances of preserving the democratic union, they must be both assertive and patient.

The western democracies must have contingency plans for when their trading partners and allies start to fall. Nearly half of the world's population resides in democracies[121]. This means there will be a lot of demand for coercing regime change in flawed democracies that are flirting with authoritarianism. Western nations have to become more comfortable with intervening in democracies and preparing for the influence campaigns. To do this, they need detailed analysis on econometrics, due process, constitutional powers, and structural defects within the branches and systems of government. Fortunately, authoritarianism seems to be spreading slowly and western nations have enough time to prepare for a new era of climate change, wealth inequality, and despotic economic superpowers[122].

Peaceful nonviolent strategies for regime change won't always be successful, and when they fail, the intelligence agencies can rely on traditional strategies for intervention. They can support armed rebellion and wars of succession or secession. Coalitions of democratic nations can seek redress through invasion and occupation as long as the outcome sought is the preservation of voting rights and civil rights. All

---

[121] Economist Intelligence Unit, "Democracy Index 2019: A year of democratic setbacks and popular protest", The Economist, Accessed Aug 6, 2020, retrieved from http://www.eiu.com/Handlers/WhitepaperHandler.as-hx?fi=Democracy-Index-2019.pdf&mode=wp&campaignid=democracyindex-2019, pp 3.

[122] Economist Intelligence Unit, "Democracy Index 2019: A year of democratic setbacks and popular protest", The Economist, Accessed Aug 6, 2020, retrieved from http://www.eiu.com/Handlers/WhitepaperHandler.as-hx?fi=Democracy-Index-2019.pdf&mode=wp&campaignid=democracyindex-2019, pp 4.

of the research made into organizing the sectarian and secular groups during rebellion will be useful when nation-building after an occupation. The coalition will work with stakeholders during the invasion and they can be rewarded by selecting their own form of government.

Intelligence departments should have intimate knowledge of the nations' public finance systems. They should know which states are net recipients and which are tax donors. They will have knowledge of which states intersect within the supply chains are for the military and law enforcement agencies. They will also have options available to form a new coalition around a new government. By selecting representational coefficients that benefit the states most needed for the institutional protest or rebellion. Analysts can look at GDP, tax revenues, personal incomes, asset ownership, and a host of other econometric data to see which states benefit most from each and then tailor a constitution that favors those democratic entitlements. By focusing on the future stakeholders, intelligence agencies can guarantee more participation and better outcomes. All of this can be accomplished prior to engagement increasing the odds of successful implementation.

The type of democracy targeted for regime change contributes a great deal to the probability of success. For example, in the United States a debt default or government shutdown could be precipitated by either chamber of the legislature. It requires majorities in both chambers to ratify a bill making it highly susceptible to disruption by an opposition party seeking regime change or independence. Even if a bill passes the bicameral process, a president could veto it, requiring a supermajority to overcome it. When political crises include threats of default and government shutdown, all agents should note the high probability of default.

Most election cycles deliver split Congresses, where a party controls at least one chamber of the legislature or the executive branch. The odds of avoiding default are only equal to a single party winning majorities in the legislature and capturing the executive branch. Any success will be fleeting, as the next midterm election will likely elevate the opposition party. Each piece of the process increases the odds of default or prolonged shut down by a sizeable amount. Although the odds may look like 25% or 12.5% superficially, they belay the underlying fact that a committed opposition party could act unilaterally from almost any position to cause a default and destroy the finances of the federal government.

In certain cases, it is worse than described. A group of just 26% members of the chamber could embargo the debt ceiling and cause a default, if the majority party does not make compromises to the minority party. An extremist movement may be able to acquire 26% of seats in a bad election year, and depending on the chamber's rules, successfully filibuster or embargo a budget or debt ceiling measure. Nothing is guaranteed during a crisis, and the worst can be expected if there are comorbidities with lack of confidence in elections, or general mistrust of government. If the default is well timed, during some other emergency, like war or depression, a small group of legislators could sabotage the war effort or force a discussion on dissolution.

Parliamentary systems cut the odds in half by virtue of electing their executive branch from the elected officers of the primary chamber. This reduces the number of moving pieces, revolving around the miasma of institutional protests, making parliaments more secure. Instead of risking a default from either of two chambers, or a veto from the executive, every threat will come exclusively from the senate, and only when the opposition party has a majority. Over time, this small structural change will result in a significant number of fewer defaults and challenges. Parliaments are therefore far more durable and flexible than Presidential systems, whose archaic structure results in more opportunities for public finance crises and threats of secession. However, parliamentary government should still be wary of an opposition party intent on secession, as they will eventually win majorities in the senate, or worse occupy the executive branch and pursue authoritarian policies. The lack of access to quick recourse, gives more opportunities for them to win the executive branch and bend it to their needs.

This inherent weakness in presidential democracies also makes them more secure against authoritarianism. The large number of checks and balances, ensures an opposition party they can eliminate the implicit advantages of a federal government by debt default or government shutdowns. An authoritarian won't likely control all chambers of government at the same time, giving the opposition party a small window to react and challenge the authoritarian policies. Presidential democracies, like the United States have impeachment proceedings, but they require majorities in both chambers to employ, and it is improbable that an opposition party controls both chambers. Political parties within Presidential systems must rely on institutional protests like debt defaults and government shutdowns because their impeachment process is slow, cumbersome, and inadequate. Parliaments have an inverse relationship, making them more susceptible to authoritarianism. There is often only one check on the executive branch, and if there is hesitation or collaboration, the fleeting opportunity could escape. The risk is overstated for Parliaments, if the party itself is able to replace the executive with a simple no confidence vote or other procedure.

Once nations are targeted for regime change, the detailed public finance knowledge and representational deficiencies can be used to organize allies acting to overthrow the government. Information will allow agencies to identify current groups that may be interested in participating and which stand to benefit from a new constitution. Even if the achieved goals are different than the stated goals, having goals will attract more participants. Agencies don't need to rely on traditional democracies with conventional representational coefficients. Econometric systems of representation can satisfy this demand and heighten interests in regime change.

The wide variety of alternate forms of democracy can all be tracked prior to engaging with the illiberal democracies. Forecasts can be made before intervention and adjusted to a moving target of econometrics and demographics during the conflict. It won't require that much work to collect and analyze the intelligence leading up to the event driving efforts to recruit allies. Most of these statistics are widely available through international institutions, universities and think tanks already, creating a platform to track the changes in terms of political representation should be an easy lift for program managers and software developers. The more information the intelligence and military agencies have, the more evidence-based decisions they can make, and the better the chances of recruiting political leaders and business leaders to the cause of regime change.

With adequate research, a suite of different classes of capitalist democracies can be offered. Different cultures may identify with different representational coefficients generating different pathways for coalitions to form. Depending on the interests of the stakeholders, legislative chambers can be based on GDP, median income, tax liabilities, asset-ownership, or other appropriate variables. Econometric systems of representation provide more solutions for more specialized groups within the nation. The newly incorporated democracy can be tailor made to fit the exact expectations of its citizens and hopefully extend the longevity of the new state. The extra effort is necessary considering the sacrifices made by enlisted and the contributions made by taxpayers. If the occupying nation can better guarantee democracy roots in the state or region, and remains viable, it is worth the additional investment in researching how different representational coefficients change the expectations of stakeholders and properties of the political systems.

Asset-based systems of representation are clearly ideal for nation-building efforts where the occupied country has significant numbers of minorities. The occupying power will likely have already reached out to form an alliance prior to the conflict. After the war, they will be stakeholders in the democracy that results from the war effort and occupation. These minority groups will favor a system of representation that gives them the benefits of collective bargaining, better role identity, and eligibility constraints for elected representatives. Democratic-Capitalism delivers on these promises when its strong anti-discriminatory properties are implemented through Asset-based representation.

Ordinary democracies may provide universal suffrage but their reliance on state-wide elections can marginalize minority voters. Demographic-majority groups might only have a small numerical advantage in population but with state-wide or nation-wide elections, they will continue to dominate elections in the executive offices and legislative chambers. Asset-based Representation has the potential to improve representation for minority groups when discrimination is present, and then ratchet down the extra-influence when normal economic outcomes are achieved.

Nations should not continue to limit themselves to traditional demographic-based democracies when many sectarian groups may be put off by the concept of majority rule and others may lack trust in contemporary parliamentary or presidential systems. Why sell only one product when a large number of more sophisticated products can be tailor made for the allies willing to risk life, liberty, and property for the cause. If nothing else, reaching out to allies beforehand, and allowing them to actively participate in the nation-building effort will strengthen their resolve for regime change. When the organic support of the people fails to deliver reforms, intelligence agencies must pursue regime change through institutional protests and nation-building.

AFTERWORD

Institutional protests are effective countermeasures against authoritarianism, but a political party is much more likely to use debt defaults and government shutdowns inappropriately and out of unjustified anger. It is like keeping a firearm in the house; it is intended to be used in self-defense but it's more likely to be used against a spouse, for suicide, or contributing to the death of a minor. Institutional Protests can be abused or misused. Most democratic nations are better off passing laws that render debt defaults and government shutdowns impossible. More stable and secure public finance systems will promote more sensible public policy and sounder elections. When there are obstacles to insurrection, the parties will make more investments into the nation. They will have a longer-term perspective and measure their rhetoric.

There are two discrete policies that will improve the durability of democratic nations. The first policy is to eliminate the requirement to authorize the sale of bonds for debts accumulated from spending previously authorized in the budget. A debt ceiling measure exposes the nation to unnecessary risk by giving authoritarians and insurrectionists and opportunity to disrupt the government. Refusing to authorize a debt ceiling will cause an immediate default, resulting in much higher debt servicing costs and far lower government revenues. A simple majority, in just one chamber of the legislature, could cause irrevocable damage to the nation, giving a rebel group the best chances by over throwing a democracy and installing their own regime. A nation can make itself less vulnerable to this form of warfare by implicitly authorizing all bonds necessary to fully fund the government after a lawful appropriations bill is ratified supporting the spending.

The second most important reform is to make the budget a living document so that political parties can't threaten government shutdowns to press for anti-democratic policies or destabilize the government. A government shutdown could last several months or years, setting the stage for a coup or revolution by state governments. By making the budget a living document, the budget for the next year uses the previously authorized spending levels, until new appropriations levels are ratified. If changes are to be made, they must be authorized by the legislature. If no changes are agreed to, the budget will continue to decrease by the rate of inflation, and when sunsetting programs expire. This will remove the threat of government shutdowns as a means for revolution, while keeping incentives for good faith negotiations on spending levels. If a nation has an inflation rate of 3%, after just 5 years, the budget will be cut by nearly 20%, at the very least. The risk of a visceral shutdown is removed while preserving the intent of the embargo. Future budget negotiations will be handled through elections.

A majority party in the legislature would be able to acquire most of the objectives of a government shutdown without a complete embargo on government.

All new expenditures require legislative approval, especially during times of war, making the appropriations susceptible to obstruction. A political party could bring an end to a domestic conflict by winning elections and preventing future appropriations. Government shutdowns provide the same utility but carry with them much more risk considering the entire federal government is shutdown. It is completely unnecessary when all new expenditures for the war can be independently embargoed. When the opposition party continues to participate in the legislative process, and seek re-election, they will tend to moderate their positions and work towards compromises.

The threat of authoritarianism grows without an easy mechanism to remove them from office, but committed parties will still have access to National Guard armies and tax protests. When a nation agrees to remove a debt ceiling measure and impose a living budget, they can also agree to more authority for governors to object to or deploy their state militias. If more of the front-line enlisted come from the counties or states, there is less of a threat from an authoritarian administration. If a threat is substantiated, more states will rally against the government, which can only rely on the enlisted from states not in open protest. States can also create the authority and infrastructure to quickly assume the revenues from an illegitimate administration. A defunded federal government, without access to a centralized military, poses less of a risk if it is compromised. More importantly, these reforms pose no direct and immediately threat to the sovereignty of the nation.

When access to debt defaults and prolong government shutdowns is denied, parties considering secession or rebellion must put more effort in organizing on the state level. They must have stronger arguments.

They must have more local support. Parties must have more resolve before they commit to the cause. It won't be a haphazard decision, whose consequences are far reaching and irreversible. Political parties will have to adapt their public policy to the expectations of future generations, in order to remain competitive in elections. Political parties naturally moderate their positions when they are more concerned with performance in subsequent elections. Even if mistakes are made, they can be repaired rather easily. By relying on tax protests and state militias, democratic parties can still take up arms against usurpers and authoritarians while removing the persistent threat debt defaults and government shutdowns bring with them.

Bibliography

Amadeo, Kimberly, (2020, March 3). "Current Federal Mandatory Spending". The Balance. Retrieved from https://www.thebalance.com/current-federal-mandatory-spending-3305772.

Amadeo, Kimberly (2020, June 28). "Current US Federal Government Spending". The Balance. Retrieved from https://www.the-balance.com/current-u-s-federal-government-spending-3305763.

Amadeo, Kimberly, (2020, July 15). "Cost of Iraq War, Its Timeline, and the Economic Impact". The Balance. Retrieved from https://www.thebalance.com/cost-of-iraq-war-timeline-economic-impact-3306301.

Arreguin-Toft, Ivan (2001). "How the Weak Win Wars: A Theory of Asymmetric Conflict". International Security, Vol. 26, No. 1.

Barroso, Amanda, (2019, Sept 10). "The changing profile of the U.S. military: Smaller in size, more diverse, more women in leadership". Pew Research Center. Retrieved from https://www.pewresearch.org/fact-tank/2019/09/10/the-changing-profile-of-the-u-s-military/.

Belasco, Amy, (2009, July 2). "Troop Levels in the Afghan and Iraq Wars, FY2001-FY2012: Cost and Other Potential Issues". Congressional Research Service, July 2, 2009. Retrieved from https://fas.org/sgp/crs/natsec/-R40682.pdf.

Camera, Lauren, (2020, Oct. 20). "Billion in Foreign Aid to Colleges and Universities Goes Undetected". U.S. News. Retrieved from https://www.usnews.com/-news/-education-news/articles/2020-10-20/billions-in-foreign-aid-to-colleges-and-universities-goes-undetected

Cancian, Mark, (2019, October 15). "U.S. Military Forces in FY 2020: Arm". Center for Strategic & International Studies. Retrieved from https://www.csis.org/-analysis/us-military-forces-fy-2020-army.

Center on Budget and Policy Priorities, (2020, April 9). "Policy Basics: Where Do Our Federal Tax Dollars Go?", Center on Budget and Policy Priorities. Retrieved from https://www.cbpp.org/research/-federal-budget/policy-basics-where-do-our-fed-eral-tax-dollars-go.

CFR.org Editors, (2020, July 13). "Demographics of the U.S. Military". Council on Foreign Relations. Retrieved from https://www.cfr.org/backgrounder/demo-graphics-us-military.

Chafetz, J. (2011). "The Unconstitutionality or the Filibuster". Connecticut Law Review, Vol 43, No. 4, pp. 1003-1040, May 2011. Retrieved from https://papers.-ssrn.com/sol3/-papers.-cfm?abstract_id=1730782

Cillizza, Chris, (2019, Oct 9). "The 2019 federal deficit is almost $1 trillion". No one seems to care. CNN. Retrieved from https://www.cnn.com-/2019/10/09/politics/budget-deficit-trump/index.html.

Congressional Research Service, (2018, Dec 10). "Shutdown of the Federal Government: Causes, Processes, and Effects". Congressional Research Service. RL34680. Retrieved from https://fas.org/sgp/crs/misc-/RL34680.pdf.

Cox, Jeff, (2013, Oct 10). "What's the worst that could happen? 7 debt-default doomsday scenarios". NBC News. Retrieved from https://www.nbcnews.com/-businessmain/whats-worst-could-happen-7-debt default-doomsday-scenarios-8C11366851.

Desilver, Drew, (2019, July 24). "5 facts about the national debt". Pew Research Center. Retrieved from https://www.pewresearch.org/fact-tank/2019-/07/24/facts-about-the-national-debt/.

Economist Intelligence Unit, (2020). "Democracy Index 2019: A year of democratic setbacks and popular protest". The Economist. Retrieved from http://www.eiu.c-om/Handlers/WhitepaperHandler.ashx?fi=Democracy-Index-2019.pdf&mode=wp&campaignid=dem-ocracyindex2019

Editors of Encyclopedia Britannica (2020, July 17). "United States Presidential Election Results". Encyclopedia Britannica. Retrieved from https://www.britannica-.com/topic/United-States-Presidential-Election-Results-1788863.

Goldstein, Steven, (2014, Nov 17). "A majority of Americans make less than $20 per hour". MarketWatch. Retrieved from https://www.marketwatch.com-/story/a-majority-of-americans-make-less-than-20-per-hour-2014-11-14.

Goldstein, Steven, (2019, April 22). "Social Security costs to exceed revenue next year, trustee report shows". MarketWatch. Retrieved from https://www.mark-etwatch.com/story/social-security-costs-to-exceed-revenue-next-year-trustee-report-shows-2019-04-22.

Governing, (2020, Aug 16). "Military Active-Duty Personnel, Civilians by State". Governing. Retrieved from https://www.governing.com/gov-data/public-workforce-salaries/military-civilian-active-duty-employee-workforce-numbers-by-state.html

Gruber, Johnathan. "Public Finance and Public Policy". New York: Worth Publishers, 2013.

Guzman, Gloria, (2019, Sept). "Household Income: 2018". Census.gov. Retrieved from https://www.census-s.gov/content/dam/Census/library/publications/2019/acs/acsbr18-01.pdf.

Hendricks, Scotty (2018, Nov 18). "What would happen if America defaulted on its debt?". Big Think. Retrieved from https://bigthink.com/politics-current-affairs/wh-at-if-the-government-defaults.

History, Art & Archives, (2020, July 11). "Party Divisions of the House of Representatives, 1789 to Present". U.S. House of Representatives. Retrieved from https://history.house.gov/Institution/Party-Divisions/Party-Divisions/.

Horowitz, Juliana Menasce, Iglienik, Ruth, and Kochar, Rakesh, (2020, Jan 9). "Trends in income and wealth inequality". Pew Research Center. Retrieved from https://www.pewsocialtrends.org/2020/01/09/trends-in-income-and-wealth-inequality/.

Infoplease Staff, (2020, March 17). "Timeline of U.S. Government Shutdowns". Infoplease. Retrieved from https://www.infoplease.com/history/us/timeline-of-us-government-shutdowns.

Internal Revenue Service, (2018, March). "Data Book, 2017". Internal Revenue Service, Publication 55B.

Keating, Christopher, Dec 10, 2020. "Quinnipiac Poll: 77% of Republicans believe there was widespread fraud in the presidential election; 60% overall consider Joe Biden's victory legitimate". Hartford Courant. Retrieved from https://www.courant.com/politics/hc-pol-q-poll-republicans-believe-fraud-20201210-pcie3uqqvrhyvnt7geohhsyepe-story.html

Mishel, Lawrence, Gould Elise, Biven Josh, (2015, Jan 6). "Wage Stagnation in Nine Charts". Economic Policy Institute. Retrieved from https://www.epi.org/publication/charting-wage-stagnation/.

Newport, Frank (2013, Feb 8). "Democrats Racially Diverse; Republicans Mostly White". Gallup. Retrieved from https://news.gallup.com/poll/160373/democrats-racially-diverse-republicans-mostly-white.aspx.

Office of Justice Programs, (2020, Aug 11). "Federal Law Enforcement". Bureau of Justice. Retrieved from https://www.bjs.gov/index.cfm?ty=tp&tid=74

Pattison, David, (2015). "Social Security Trust Fund Cash Flows and Reserves". Social Security Administration. Retrieved from https://www.ssa.gov/policy/docs/ssb/v75n1/v75n1p1.html.

Pew Research Center, (2020, June 2). "U.S. Politics & Policy". Pew Research Center. Retrieved from https://w-ww.pewresearch.org/politics/2020/06/02/-democratic-edge-in-party-identification-narrows-slightly/

Polk, William. "Violent Politics. New York: Harper Collins, 2007.

Polston Jr , Dudley L. and Saenz, Rogelio. "U.S. whites will soon be the minority in number, but not power". Baltimore Sun, Aug 8, 2017, retrieved from https://www.baltimoresun.com/opinion/op-ed/bs-ed-op-0809-minority-majority-20170808-story.html.

Przeworksi, Adam. "Minimalist Conception of Democracy: A Defense". In Democracy's Value edited by Shapiro, I. and Hacker-Cordon, C. Cambridge: Cambridge University, 1999.

Robson, David, (2019, May 13). "The '3.5% rule': How a small minority can change the world". BBC. Retrieved from https://www.bbc.com/future/article/20190513-it-only-takes-35-of-people-to-change-the-world.

Romig, Kathleen (2016, Sept 26). "Increasing Payroll Taxes Would Strengthen Social Security". Center on Budget and Policy Priorities. Center on Budget and Policy Priorities. Retrieved from https://www.cbpp.org/-research/social-security/increasing-payroll-taxes-would-strengthen-social-security

Social Security Resource Center, (2020, July 11). "What is the maximum amount of income that is subject to FICA taxes?". AARP. Retrieved from https://www.aar-p.org/retirement/social-security/questions-answers/maximum-amount-income-subject-to-fica-tax/.

Stolba, Stefan Lembo, (2019, Nov 18). "Median Home Value by State". Experian. Retrieved from https://www.experian.com/blogs/ask-experian/-research/median-home-values-by-state/.

Travis, Shannon, (2011, July 29). "Who is the Tea Party Caucus in the House?". CNN. Retrieved from https://politicalticker.blogs.cnn.com/2011/07/29/who-is-the-tea-party-caucus-in-the-house/.

U.S Census Bureau, (2020, Aug 14). "State Population Totals and Components of a change: 2010-2019". Retrieve from https://www2.census.gov/programs-surveys-/popest/datasets/2010-2019/national/totals/nst-est2019-alldata.csv?#

U.S. Office of Personnel Management, (2015, Sept). "Guidance for Shutdown Furloughs". Office of Personnel Management. Retrieved from https://www.opm.gov/-policy-data-oversight/pay-leave/furlough-guidance/guidance-for-shutdown-furloughs.pdf.

Vespa, j., Median, L., Armstrong, David M. (March 2018) "Demographic Turning Points for the United States: Population Projections for 2020 to 2060", p25-1144, retrieved from https://www.census.gov/content/dam-/Census/library/publications/2020/demo/p25-1144.pdf

Wasson, Donald L., (2016, April 07). "Roman Republic". Ancient History Encyclopedia. Retrieved from https://www.ancient.eu/Roman_Republic/

Weisinger, Jordan. Income-based Representation. South Carolina: KDP, 2019.

World Bank, (2020, Aug 5). "GDP Growth (Annual %) – United States", World Bank. Retrieved from https://data.worldbank.org/indicator/-NY.GDP.MK-TP.KD.ZG?locations=US.

World Bank, (2020, Aug 5). "GDP (Current US$) – United States", World Bank. Retrieved from https://data.worldbank.org/indicator/NY.GDP.MKTP.CD?locations=US

Zingher, Joshua (2018, May 22). "Whites have fled the Democratic Party. Here's how the nation got there". The Washington Post. retrieved from https://www.washingtonpost.com/news/monkey-cage/wp/2018/05/22/whites-have-fled-the-democratic-party-heres-how-the-nation-got-there/

Table 1.0 Micropolitical Binary Partition (All States)

State		% of owners	Population	Non Owners Reps	% of Non-	Owners Reps	% of Owners Chamber
New York	D	53%	19,745,289.00	34	7.75%	22	5.17%
California	D	54%	39,250,017.00	66	15.24%	45	10.37%
Nevada	D	54%	2,940,058.00	5	1.13%	3	0.78%
Hawaii	D	57%	1,428,557.00	2	0.52%	2	0.40%
Rhode Isla	D	59%	1,056,426.00	2	0.36%	1	0.31%
Oregon	D	61%	4,093,465.00	6	1.33%	5	1.23%
Massachu	D	62%	6,811,779.00	9	2.18%	9	2.07%
Washingt	D	62%	7,288,000.00	10	2.29%	10	2.24%
Colorado	D	64%	5,540,545.00	7	1.68%	8	1.74%
Illinois	D	65%	12,801,539.00	16	3.72%	18	4.12%
New Jerse	D	66%	8,944,469.00	11	2.57%	13	2.89%
Maryland	D	66%	6,016,447.00	7	1.72%	8	1.95%
Connectic	D	66%	3,576,452.00	4	1.01%	5	1.17%
Wisonsin	D	67%	5,778,708.00	7	1.61%	8	1.90%
New Mex	D	68%	2,081,015.00	2	0.57%	3	0.69%
Pennslyva	D	69%	12,784,227.00	15	3.35%	19	4.33%
Michigan	D	70%	9,928,300.00	11	2.46%	15	3.44%
Vermont	D	71%	624,594.00	1	0.15%	1	0.22%
Delaware	D	71%	952,065.00	1	0.23%	1	0.33%
New Ham	D	71%	1,334,795.00	1	0.32%	2	0.47%
Minnesot	D	71%	5,519,952.00	6	1.34%	8	1.93%
Maine	D	71%	1,331,479.00	1	0.32%	2	0.47%
Virginia	R	65%	8,411,808.00	11	2.46%	12	2.69%
Texas	R	61%	27,862,596.00	39	9.07%	36	8.39%
North Dak	R	62%	757,952.00	1	0.24%	1	0.23%
Georgia	R	62%	10,310,371.00	14	3.29%	14	3.14%
Arizona	R	62%	6,931,071.00	10	2.21%	9	2.11%
Florida	R	64%	20,612,439.00	27	6.24%	28	6.48%
North Car	R	64%	10,146,788.00	13	3.06%	14	3.20%
Alaska	R	64%	741,894.00	1	0.22%	1	0.23%
Louisiana	R	65%	4,681,666.00	6	1.39%	6	1.49%
South Dak	R	65%	865,454.00	1	0.25%	1	0.28%
Arkansas	R	65%	2,988,248.00	4	0.87%	4	0.96%
Oklahoma	R	65%	3,923,561.00	5	1.14%	5	1.26%
Ohio	R	65%	11,614,373.00	15	3.36%	16	3.74%
Tennessse	R	66%	6,651,194.00	8	1.90%	9	2.16%
Nebraska	R	66%	1,907,116.00	2	0.54%	3	0.62%
Missouri	R	66%	6,093,000.00	8	1.73%	9	1.98%
Kentucky	R	66%	4,436,974.00	5	1.25%	6	1.45%
Kansas	R	66%	2,907,289.00	4	0.82%	4	0.95%
Montana	R	67%	1,042,520.00	1	0.29%	1	0.34%
Mississipp	R	67%	2,988,726.00	4	0.82%	4	0.99%
Alabama	R	68%	4,863,300.00	6	1.31%	7	1.63%
Wyoming	R	68%	585,501.00	1	0.16%	1	0.20%
South Car	R	68%	4,961,119.00	6	1.32%	7	1.67%
Indiana	R	68%	6,633,053.00	8	1.76%	10	2.23%
Utah	R	69%	3,051,217.00	3	0.79%	5	1.04%
Idaho	R	69%	1,683,140.00	2	0.44%	2	0.57%
Iowa	R	71%	3,134,693.00	3	0.77%	5	1.09%
West Virg	R	72%	1,831,102.00	2	0.42%	3	0.65%

Table 1.1 Micropolitical Binary Partition
Republican states (alone)

State	Non Owner Reps	% of Non Owners	Owners Reps	% of Owners
Virginia	22	5.12%	23	5.20%
Texas	82	18.83%	70	16.20%
North Dakota	2	0.50%	2	0.45%
Georgia	30	6.84%	26	6.06%
Arizona	20	4.59%	18	4.08%
Florida	56	12.97%	54	12.52%
North Carolina	28	6.37%	27	6.17%
Alaska	2	0.47%	2	0.45%
Louisiana	13	2.88%	13	2.88%
South Dakota	2	0.53%	2	0.54%
Arkansas	8	1.81%	8	1.85%
Oklahoma	10	2.37%	11	2.44%
Ohio	30	6.98%	31	7.23%
Tennesssee	17	3.95%	18	4.17%
Nebraska	5	1.13%	5	1.20%
Missouri	16	3.59%	17	3.83%
Kentucky	11	2.60%	12	2.80%
Kansas	7	1.70%	8	1.84%
Montana	3	0.60%	3	0.66%
Mississippi	7	1.69%	8	1.92%
Alabama	12	2.71%	14	3.14%
Wyoming	1	0.33%	2	0.38%
South Carolina	12	2.75%	14	3.22%
Indiana	16	3.67%	19	4.31%
Utah	7	1.65%	9	2.00%
Idaho	4	0.91%	5	1.11%
Iowa	7	1.60%	9	2.11%
West Virginia	4	0.88%	5	1.26%

Table 1.2 Micropolitical Binary Partition
Democratic States (alone)

State	Non Owner Reps	% Non-owner	Owners Reps	% Owners
New York	32	14.94%	47	10.72%
California	64	29.38%	94	21.50%
Nevada	5	2.18%	7	1.62%
Hawaii	2	1.00%	4	0.83%
Rhode Island	2	0.70%	3	0.64%
Oregon	6	2.57%	11	2.56%
Massachusetts	9	4.21%	19	4.30%
Washington	10	4.42%	20	4.65%
Colorado	7	3.24%	16	3.61%
Illinois	16	7.17%	37	8.54%
New Jersey	11	4.96%	26	6.00%
Maryland	7	3.31%	18	4.05%
Connecticut	4	1.95%	11	2.42%
Wisconsin	7	3.10%	17	3.95%
New Mexico	2	1.09%	6	1.44%
Pennslyvania	14	6.46%	39	8.98%
Michigan	10	4.74%	31	7.14%
Vermont	1	0.30%	2	0.45%
Delaware	1	0.45%	3	0.69%
New Hampsire	1	0.63%	4	0.97%
Minnesota	6	2.59%	17	4.00%
Maine	1	0.62%	4	0.97%

Table 1.3 Macropolitical Binary (by State) – Lower Chamber

State	Party	Proportion of ownership	Chamber	# of Reps
New York	D	0.53	Lower	26
California	D	0.54	Lower	51
Nevada	D	0.54	Lower	4
Hawaii	D	0.57	Lower	2
Rhode Island	D	0.59	Lower	1
Oregon	D	0.61	Lower	5
Massachusetts	D	0.62	Lower	9
Washington	D	0.62	Lower	10
Colorado	D	0.64	Lower	7
Texas	R	0.61	Lower	36
North Dakota	R	0.62	Lower	1
Georgia	R	0.62	Lower	13
Arizona	R	0.62	Lower	9
Florida	R	0.64	Lower	27
North Carolina	R	0.64	Lower (9)	13

Table 1.4 Macropolitical Binary (by State) – Upper Chamber

State	Party	Proportion of Ownership	Chmaber	# of Reps
North Carolina	R	0.64	Upper (5)	13
Illinois	D	0.65	Upper	17
New Jersey	D	0.66	Upper	12
Maryland	D	0.66	Upper	8
Connecticut	D	0.66	Upper	5
Wisconsin	D	0.67	Upper	8
New Mexico	D	0.68	Upper	3
Pennslyvania	D	0.69	Upper	17
Michigan	D	0.70	Upper	13
Vermont	D	0.71	Upper	1
Delaware	D	0.71	Upper	1
New Hampsire	D	0.71	Upper	2
Minnesota	D	0.71	Upper	7
Maine	D	0.71	Upper	2
Alaska	R	0.64	Upper	1
Louisiana	R	0.65	Upper	6
South Dakota	R	0.65	Upper	1
Virginia	R	0.65	Upper	11
Arkansas	R	0.65	Upper	4
Oklahoma	R	0.65	Upper	5
Ohio	R	0.65	Upper	15
Tennesssee	R	0.66	Upper	9
Nebraska	R	0.66	Upper	2
Missouri	R	0.66	Upper	8
Kentucky	R	0.66	Upper	6
Kansas	R	0.66	Upper	4
Montana	R	0.67	Upper	1
Mississippi	R	0.67	Upper	4
Alabama	R	0.68	Upper	6
Wyoming	R	0.68	Upper	1
South Carolina	R	0.68	Upper	6
Indiana	R	0.68	Upper	9
Utah	R	0.69	Upper	4
Idaho	R	0.69	Upper	2
Iowa	R	0.71	Upper	4
West Virginia	R	0.72	Upper	2

Table 1.5 Demographic-based Representational Coefficient

(Approximation of US system – 2020 Demographics)

State	Population	Demographic
New York	19,745,289	27
California	39,250,017	53
Nevada	2,940,058	4
Hawaii	1,428,557	2
Rhode Island	1,056,426	1
Oregon	4,093,465	6
Massachusetts	6,811,779	9
Washington	7,288,000	10
Colorado	5,540,545	7
Illinois	12,801,539	17
New Jersey	8,944,469	12
Maryland	6,016,447	8
Connecticut	3,576,452	5
Wisconsin	5,778,708	8
New Mexico	2,081,015	3
Pennslyvania	12,784,227	17
Michigan	9,928,300	13
Vermont	624,594	1
Delaware	952,065	1
New Hampsire	1,334,795	2
Minnesota	5,519,952	7
Maine	1,331,479	2
Texas	27,862,596	38
North Dakota	757,952	1
Georgia	10,310,371	14
Arizona	6,931,071	9
Florida	20,612,439	28
North Carolina	10,146,788	14
Alaska	741,894	1
Louisiana	4,681,666	6
South Dakota	865,454	1
Virginia	8,411,808	11
Arkansas	2,988,248	4
Oklahoma	3,923,561	5
Ohio	11,614,373	16
Tennesssee	6,651,194	9
Nebraska	1,907,116	3
Missouri	6,093,000	8
Kentucky	4,436,974	6
Kansas	2,907,289	4
Montana	1,042,520	1
Mississippi	2,988,726	4
Alabama	4,863,300	7
Wyoming	585,501	1
South Carolina	4,961,119	7
Indiana	6,633,053	9
Utah	3,051,217	4
Idaho	1,683,140	2
Iowa	3,134,693	4
West Virginia	1,831,102	2
	322,446,343	435
	741255.961	

Table 1.6 Home-ownership Demographics

Territory	Total	White alone	Black alone	AIAN alone	Asian alone	NHPI alone	Some other race alone	Two or more races	Hispanic	White alone, not Hispanic
United States	66.2	71.3	46.3	55.5	53.4	45	40.5	46.3	45.7	72.4
Alabama	72.5	77.8	57.6	70.5	48.4	44.8	32.2	61.9	43.9	78
Alaska	62.5	65.7	33.7	59.5	50.1	34.3	42	51.1	42.6	66
Arizona	68	71.3	44	60.4	58.3	48.9	52.5	52.1	55	72.8
Arkansas	69.4	73.4	50.1	58.3	50.7	36.1	37.3	57.6	39.6	73.7
California	56.9	62.6	38.8	46.1	55.4	44.4	40.5	43.5	43.7	64.9
Colorado	67.3	70.1	44.7	50.1	57	48.8	49.4	50.9	53	71.2
Connecticut	66.8	72.5	36.5	44.2	48.1	43.5	22	38.6	28.1	73.9
Delaware	72.3	78.6	50.4	64.3	52.4	44.2	39	50.6	43	79.2
District of Columbia	40.8	47.2	38.8	33	24.5	18.9	20	29.6	24.2	48.5
Florida	70.1	74.1	50.2	60.3	60.6	49.3	46.4	52	55.8	76.4
Georgia	67.5	75.3	50.8	56.6	55.4	46.1	32.5	49.3	37.4	76.1
Hawaii	56.5	48.8	15.7	32.8	69	46.7	26	49.7	36.6	49.3
Idaho	72.4	73.6	42.9	59.9	63.2	53.4	51.1	57.9	52.1	74
Illinois	67.3	73.5	42.2	50.6	54.6	44.5	46.9	47.2	48.6	74.7
Indiana	71.4	74.6	45.2	56.5	46	48.8	43.8	51.8	48.6	74.9
Iowa	72.3	73.7	37.1	46.3	45.8	37	43.6	47.7	46.9	73.9
Kansas	69.2	72	43.9	54	50.8	45.3	49.1	52.3	50.9	72.4
Kentucky	70.8	73.6	41.4	52.6	42.8	37.3	24.3	51.2	36.4	73.8
Louisiana	67.9	75.4	51.8	68.6	53.4	46.3	41.9	55.2	51.4	75.7
Maine	71.6	72.1	32.6	52.5	46.9	50.5	37.8	51.8	46.2	72.2
Maryland	67.7	75.4	51.3	58.3	60.5	51.3	43.6	50.9	48	75.8
Massachusetts	61.7	65.9	31.6	37.7	41.6	36.6	20.9	33.8	21.8	66.8
Michigan	73.8	78.4	50.7	60.5	50.4	52.4	49.9	56.6	54.9	78.7
Minnesota	74.6	77.2	31.5	50.1	53.3	46.8	38.1	46	42.9	77.5
Mississippi	72.3	78.5	60.7	66.8	51.2	56.9	29.2	59	45.4	78.7
Missouri	70.3	73.7	47.2	57.7	47.7	44.7	41.9	53.4	48.9	73.9
Montana	69.1	70.5	33	49.6	47.8	48.9	44.6	54.3	47.5	70.7
Nebraska	67.4	69.7	39.2	36.9	44.3	37.6	43.9	42.4	46.2	70
Nevada	60.9	64.3	39.8	54.6	58.9	42.6	44	48.5	46	65.9
New Hampshire	69.7	70.6	35.9	47.6	44.2	52.1	27.5	48.4	36.4	70.8
New Jersey	65.6	73.1	40.3	45.6	54.7	40.6	28.3	38.9	33.2	75.7
New Mexico	70	71.9	45.8	68.9	54.5	55.2	66.6	61.6	69.3	71.9
New York	53	62.3	29.1	35.4	39.8	29.6	15.9	28.5	19.6	65
North Carolina	69.4	75.1	52.5	70.4	52.5	41	28.2	46.8	31.3	75.7
North Dakota	66.6	68.1	17.8	44.9	36.2	37	31.9	44.6	38.7	68.2
Ohio	69.1	73.2	42.6	51.8	47.5	44.8	42.2	47.9	47.5	73.4
Oklahoma	68.4	71.9	44	64.2	48.2	43.8	43.9	63.1	45.7	72.3
Oregon	64.3	66.4	37.4	48.3	55.6	34.3	35	47.3	37	66.9
Pennsylvania	71.3	74.6	49.5	52.2	49.1	51.8	40.4	48.7	43.5	74.8
Rhode Island	60	64.1	28.2	31.1	41.1	30.9	23.1	33.6	21.3	65.1
South Carolina	72.2	77.2	60.9	62.7	54.4	45.7	31.5	55	39.4	77.5
South Dakota	68.2	70.5	28.1	38.8	38.9	33.3	31.6	50	40.1	70.6
Tennessee	69.9	74.1	50.5	55.9	50.5	42.3	27.1	52.4	35.8	74.4
Texas	63.8	68.7	46.4	56.5	53.1	46.5	50.7	52.3	56.1	70.8
Utah	71.5	73.3	39.6	53.3	60.4	55.8	49.7	50.2	50.7	74
Vermont	70.6	71.1	33.1	50.1	44.1	40.5	42.6	53.8	50.9	71.2
Virginia	68.1	73.5	51.1	58	57	49.1	37.2	47.7	44.3	74
Washington	64.6	67.4	37.4	50.8	56.9	41.1	40.2	46.7	41.6	67.9
West Virginia	75.2	76.3	49.8	60.8	49.1	54	44.1	59.7	60.3	76.3
Wisconsin	68.4	71.4	32.5	47.5	42.7	45.8	33.1	42.7	37.5	71.7
Wyoming	70	71	41.4	54.5	53.9	47.9	54	58.3	58.6	71.3

ASSET-BASED REPRESENTATION

Table 1.7 Value Rep. Coefficient (Republican)

State	Median Value	Ownership rate	Population	Median Value X Population	MxP Reps	Adjusted MvXP	Adj MxP reps
Virginia	297000	65%	8411808	2,498,306,976,000	18	1,623,899,534,400	18
Texas	214763	61%	27862596	5,983,854,704,748	44	3,656,135,224,601	42
North Dakota	190000	62%	757952	144,010,880,000	1	88,854,712,960	1
Georgia	166900	62%	10310371	1,720,800,919,900	13	1,063,454,968,498	12
Arizona	209000	62%	6931071	1,448,593,839,000	11	896,679,586,341	10
Florida	185000	64%	20612439	3,813,301,215,000	28	2,432,886,175,170	28
North Carolina	177000	64%	10146788	1,795,981,476,000	13	1,147,632,163,164	13
Alaska	291530	64%	741894	216,284,357,820	2	138,205,704,647	2
Louisiana	162000	65%	4681666	758,429,892,000	6	489,945,710,232	6
South Dakota	144532	65%	865454	125,085,797,528	1	81,305,768,393	1
Arkansas	145000	65%	2988248	433,295,960,000	3	282,508,965,920	3
Oklahoma	130500	65%	3923561	512,024,710,500	4	334,352,135,957	4
Ohio	130000	65%	11614373	1,509,868,490,000	11	987,453,992,460	11
Tennesssee	145000	66%	6651194	964,423,130,000	7	634,590,419,540	7
Nebraska	152000	66%	1907116	289,881,632,000	2	191,031,995,488	2
Missouri	159668	66%	6093000	972,857,124,000	7	643,058,558,964	7
Kentucky	140000	66%	4436974	621,176,360,000	5	411,839,926,680	5
Kansas	157938	66%	2907289	459,171,410,082	3	304,889,816,294	3
Montana	230608	67%	1042520	240,413,452,160	2	160,355,772,591	2
Mississippi	207783	67%	2988726	621,006,454,458	5	418,558,350,305	5
Alabama	143500	68%	4863300	697,883,550,000	5	473,862,930,450	5
Wyoming	219450	68%	585501	128,488,194,450	1	87,371,972,226	1
South Carolina	161500	68%	4961119	801,220,718,500	6	545,631,309,299	6
Indiana	163233	68%	6633053	1,082,733,140,349	8	738,424,001,718	8
Utah	258665	69%	3051217	789,243,045,305	6	543,788,458,215	6
Idaho	210489	69%	1683140	354,282,455,460	3	244,454,894,267	3
Iowa	144300	71%	3134693	452,336,199,900	3	319,801,693,329	4
West Virginia	122550	72%	1831102	224,401,550,100	2	162,242,320,722	2
		66%	162618165	29,659,357,635,260	217	19,103,217,062,831	217
			749392.4654	136,679,067,444		88,033,258,354	

Table 1.8 Value Per Capita Representation (Republican)

State	Per Capita GDP	MxP Reps	MxP per Capita	Adj MxP reps	Adj Per Capita
Virginia	56938	18	1040748.999	18	1050302.958
Texas	61682	44	2700458.328	42	2561733.34
North Dakota	70991	1	74799.13767	1	71653.43014
Georgia	50186	13	631845.9482	12	606254.4094
Arizona	44161	11	468040.5985	10	449810.3098
Florida	44267	28	1235034.801	28	1223362.333
North Carolina	48496	13	637244.0147	13	632210.717
Alaska	74422	2	117767.2249	2	116837.0357
Louisiana	51729	6	287043.3682	6	287895.758
South Dakota	52913	1	48424.86072	1	48869.39554
Arkansas	39580	3	125475.352	3	127016.8239
Oklahoma	50876	4	190590.7734	4	193228.1002
Ohio	52664	11	581769.5105	11	590723.0748
Tennesssee	48440	7	341798.1794	7	349181.2128
Nebraska	59386	2	125951.332	2	128867.5019
Missouri	47407	7	337434.5358	7	346294.9989
Kentucky	42386	5	192635.0661	5	198291.5032
Kansas	53528	3	179826.5652	3	185386.096
Montana	44145	2	77649.43121	2	80411.7184
Mississippi	35015	5	159091.962	5	166480.4974
Alabama	41389	5	211332.3041	5	222787.5373
Wyoming	67915	1	63845.00487	1	67404.83772
South Carolina	41457	6	243023.3682	6	256951.0389
Indiana	49321	8	390707.0937	8	413705.1254
Utah	51407	6	296845.874	6	317545.1391
Idaho	40566	3	105150.1328	3	112645.5777
Iowa	55051	3	182190.0062	4	199985.8161
West Virginia	40265	2	66107.62411	2	74207.03455
		217		217	
Pre Capita	50592.25		51211.20459		51060.10747

Table 1.9 Value Rep. Coefficient (Democrat)

State	Median Value	Ownership Rates	Population	Median Value X Population	MxP Reps	Adjusted MvXP	Adj MxP reps
New York	247,000	53%	19,745,289	4,877,086,383,000	24	2,589,732,869,373	21
California	422,500	54%	39,250,017	16,583,132,182,500	81	8,888,558,849,820	73
Nevada	216,000	54%	2,940,058	635,052,528,000	3	342,928,365,120	3
Hawaii	485,000	57%	1,428,557	692,850,145,000	3	392,153,182,070	3
Rhode Island	230,000	59%	1,056,426	242,977,980,000	1	143,357,008,200	1
Oregon	275,000	61%	4,093,465	1,125,702,875,000	6	687,804,456,625	6
Massachusetts	339,900	62%	6,811,779	2,315,323,682,100	11	1,428,554,711,856	12
Washington	299,000	62%	7,288,000	2,179,112,000,000	11	1,359,765,888,000	11
Colorado	300,000	64%	5,540,545	1,662,163,500,000	8	1,058,798,149,500	9
Illinois	185,000	65%	12,801,539	2,368,284,715,000	12	1,546,489,918,895	13
New Jersey	265,000	66%	8,944,469	2,370,284,285,000	12	1,554,906,490,960	13
Maryland	242,000	66%	6,016,447	1,455,980,174,000	7	959,490,934,666	8
Connecticut	227,500	66%	3,576,452	813,642,830,000	4	538,631,553,460	4
Wisonsin	167,200	67%	5,778,708	966,199,977,600	5	645,421,585,037	5
New Mexico	196,330	68%	2,081,015	408,565,674,950	2	275,781,830,591	2
Pennslyvania	161,000	69%	12,784,227	2,058,260,547,000	10	1,414,024,995,789	12
Michigan	134,900	70%	9,928,300	1,339,327,670,000	7	942,886,679,680	8
Vermont	195,000	71%	624,594	121,795,830,000	1	86,109,651,810	1
Delaware	212,000	71%	952,065	201,837,780,000	1	142,901,148,240	1
New Hampsire	232,000	71%	1,334,795	309,672,440,000	2	219,557,759,960	2
Minnesota	219,900	71%	5,519,952	1,213,837,444,800	6	860,610,748,363	7
Maine	235,220	71%	1,331,479	313,190,490,380	2	222,365,248,170	2
		64%	159,828,178	44,254,281,134,330	217	26,300,832,026,185	217
			736535.382	203,936,779,421		121,201,990,904	

Table 1.10 Value Per Capita Rep (Democratic)

State	Per Capita GDP	MxP Reps	MxP per Capita	Adj MxP reps	Adj Per Capita
New York	75131	24	1796735	21	1605330.232
California	70622	81	5742632	73	5179187.226
Nevada	50043	3	155832	3	141591.438
Hawaii	58981	3	200381	3	190835.0404
Rhode Island	51963	1	61911	1	61461.53344
Oregon	52726	6	291040	6	299212.7234
Massachusetts	75258	11	854415	12	887033.0405
Washington	69761	11	745413	11	782649.0919
Colorado	61311	8	499708	9	535601.543
Illinois	61713	12	716663	13	787433.7018
New Jersey	63495	12	737980	13	814580.5767
Maryland	61926	7	442113	8	490234.8153
Connecticut	69789	4	278436	4	310148.0199
Wisonsin	52534	5	248893	5	279752.6451
New Mexico	46304	2	92765	2	105359.671
Pennslyvania	56868	10	573948	12	663460.8298
Michigan	47448	7	311608	8	369120.0684
Vermont	48855	1	29177	1	34709.71894
Delaware	64985	1	64316	1	76619.4602
New Hampsire	57272	2	86966	2	103748.395
Minnesota	60066	6	357515	7	426506.5683
Maine	43541	2	66867	2	79883.21973
		217	14355314	217	14,224,460
Per Capita	59118		66154		65551

Table 1.11 Value Rep Coefficient (all)

State	Party	Median Value	Ownership Rate	Population	Median Value X Population	MxP Reps	Adjusted MvXP	Adj MxP reps
New York	D	247,000	0.53	19,745,289	4,877,086,383,000	29	2,589,732,869,373	25
California	D	422,500	0.54	39,250,017	16,583,132,182,500	98	8,888,558,849,820	85
Nevada	D	216,000	0.54	2,940,058	635,052,528,000	4	342,928,365,120	3
Hawaii	D	485,000	0.57	1,428,557	692,850,145,000	4	392,153,182,070	4
Rhode Island	D	230,000	0.59	1,056,426	242,977,980,000	1	143,357,008,200	1
Oregon	D	275,000	0.61	4,093,465	1,125,702,875,000	7	687,804,456,625	7
Massachusett:	D	339,900	0.62	6,811,779	2,315,323,682,100	14	1,428,554,711,856	14
Washington	D	299,000	0.62	7,288,000	2,179,112,000,000	13	1,359,765,888,000	13
Colorado	D	300,000	0.64	5,540,545	1,662,163,500,000	10	1,058,798,149,500	10
Virginia	R	297,000	0.65	8,411,808	2,498,306,976,000	15	1,623,899,534,400	16
Illinois	D	185,000	0.65	12,801,539	2,368,284,715,000	14	1,546,489,918,895	15
New Jersey	D	265,000	0.66	8,944,469	2,370,284,285,000	14	1,554,906,490,960	15
Maryland	D	242,000	0.66	6,016,447	1,455,980,174,000	9	959,490,934,666	9
Connecticut	D	227,500	0.66	3,576,452	813,642,830,000	5	538,631,553,460	5
Wisonsin	D	167,200	0.67	5,778,708	966,199,977,600	6	645,421,585,037	6
New Mexico	D	196,330	0.68	2,081,015	408,565,674,950	2	275,781,830,591	3
Pennslyvania	D	161,000	0.69	12,784,227	2,058,260,547,000	12	1,414,024,995,789	14
Michigan	D	134,900	0.70	9,928,300	1,339,327,670,000	8	942,886,679,680	9
Vermont	D	195,000	0.71	624,594	121,795,830,000	1	86,109,651,810	1
Delaware	D	212,000	0.71	952,065	201,837,780,000	1	142,901,148,240	1
New Hampsir(	D	232,000	0.71	1,334,795	309,672,440,000	2	219,557,759,960	2
Minnesota	D	219,900	0.71	5,519,952	1,213,837,444,800	7	860,610,748,363	8
Maine	D	235,220	0.71	1,331,479	313,190,490,380	2	222,365,248,170	2
Texas	R	214,763	0.61	27,862,596	5,983,854,704,748	35	3,656,135,224,601	35
North Dakota	R	190,000	0.62	757,952	144,010,880,000	1	88,854,712,960	1
Georgia	R	166,900	0.62	10,310,371	1,720,800,919,900	10	1,063,454,968,498	10
Arizona	R	209,000	0.62	6,931,071	1,448,593,839,000	9	896,679,586,341	9
Florida	R	185,000	0.64	20,612,439	3,813,301,215,000	22	2,432,886,175,170	23
North Carolina	R	177,000	0.64	10,146,788	1,795,981,476,000	11	1,147,632,163,164	11
Alaska	R	291,530	0.64	741,894	216,284,357,820	1	138,205,704,647	1
Louisiana	R	162,000	0.65	4,681,666	758,429,892,000	4	489,945,710,232	5
South Dakota	R	144,532	0.65	865,454	125,085,797,528	1	81,305,768,393	1
Arkansas	R	145,000	0.65	2,988,248	433,295,960,000	3	282,508,965,920	3
Oklahoma	R	130,500	0.65	3,923,561	512,024,710,500	3	334,352,135,957	3
Ohio	R	130,000	0.65	11,614,373	1,509,868,490,000	9	987,453,992,460	9
Tennesssee	R	145,000	0.66	6,651,194	964,423,130,000	6	634,590,419,540	6
Nebraska	R	152,000	0.66	1,907,116	289,881,632,000	2	191,031,995,488	2
Missouri	R	159,668	0.66	6,093,000	972,857,124,000	6	643,058,558,964	6
Kentucky	R	140,000	0.66	4,436,974	621,176,360,000	4	411,839,926,680	4
Kansas	R	157,938	0.66	2,907,289	459,171,410,082	3	304,889,816,294	3
Montana	R	230,608	0.67	1,042,520	240,413,452,160	1	160,355,772,591	2
Mississippi	R	207,783	0.67	2,988,726	621,006,454,458	4	418,558,350,305	4
Alabama	R	143,500	0.68	4,863,300	697,883,550,000	4	473,862,930,450	5
Wyoming	R	219,450	0.68	585,501	128,488,194,450	1	87,371,972,226	1
South Carolina	R	161,500	0.68	4,961,119	801,220,718,500	5	545,631,309,299	5
Indiana	R	163,233	0.68	6,633,053	1,082,733,140,349	6	738,424,001,718	7
Utah	R	258,665	0.69	3,051,217	789,243,045,305	5	543,788,458,215	5
Idaho	R	210,489	0.69	1,683,140	354,282,455,460	2	244,454,894,267	2
Iowa	R	144,300	0.71	3,134,693	452,336,199,900	3	319,801,693,329	3
West Virginia	R	122,550	0.72	1,831,102	224,401,550,100	1	162,747,320,722	2
			0.65	322,446,343	73,913,638,769,590	435	45,404,048,080,016	435
				742963.924	169,916,410,965		104,377,124,343	

Table 1.12 Value Per Capita Rep (all)

State	Per Capita GDP	Adj Per Capita	MxP per Capita	Represented Per Capita
New York	75131	1864098.302	2156474	1996710
California	70622	6014036.189	6892412	3730887
Nevada	50043	164414.9931	187033	198030
Hawaii	58981	221596.3218	240501	113408
Rhode Island	51963	71368.7052	74306	73887
Oregon	52726	347443.7336	349312	290501
Massachusetts	75258	1030016.598	1025484	689994
Washington	69761	908806.6826	894658	684311
Colorado	61311	621936.7869	599759	457218
Virginia	56938	885841.5316	837168	644650
Illinois	61713	914362.5384	860152	1063337
New Jersey	63495	945885.3007	885737	764410
Maryland	61926	569257.2582	530632	501471
Connecticut	69789	360141.7238	334184	335948
Wisonsin	52534	324846.826	298725	408605
New Mexico	46304	122342.9172	111338	129696
Pennslyvania	56868	770406.1016	688863	978531
Michigan	47448	428619.6565	373998	634052
Vermont	48855	40304.68425	35019	41071
Delaware	64985	88969.98434	77193	83274
New Hampsire	57272	120471.9148	104378	102894
Minnesota	60066	495256.461	429095	446269
Maine	43541	92759.8392	80255	78031
Texas	61682	2160604.963	2172222	2313195
North Dakota	70991	60433.59565	60168	72423
Georgia	50186	511324.2139	508251	696449
Arizona	44161	379376.8746	376487	411976
Florida	44267	1031802.447	993450	1228123
North Carolina	48496	533216.1595	512593	662318
Alaska	74422	98542.13762	94731	74315
Louisiana	51729	242815.6725	230895	325962
South Dakota	52913	41217.19342	38952	61637
Arkansas	39580	107127.9262	100931	159193
Oklahoma	50876	162971.5263	153309	268674
Ohio	52664	498224.8494	467970	823269
Tennesssee	48440	294504.7597	274939	433647
Nebraska	59386	108688.8162	101314	152438
Missouri	47407	292070.4828	271429	388782
Kentucky	42386	167242.0776	154954	253129
Kansas	53528	156357.4604	144651	209460
Montana	44145	67820.46953	62460	61944
Mississippi	35015	140412.1902	127972	140855
Alabama	41389	187902.4063	169994	270924
Wyoming	67915	56850.26802	51356	53521
South Carolina	41457	216716.4245	195486	276828
Indiana	49321	348925.2115	314281	440329
Utah	51407	267822.4127	238780	211119
Idaho	40566	95006.99797	84582	91900
Iowa	55051	168671.087	146552	232270
West Virginia	40265	62587.34455	53176	99237
		25,862,421	26168561	24861100
		59454	60158	57152

Table 1.13 2000 Micropolitical Demographics and Ownership

Race	% of Population	Ownership Rate	% of Owners Chamber	% of Non- owners Chamber
White	69.10%	72.40%	78.22%	54.89%
Black	12.90%	46.30%	9.34%	19.94%
Asian	4.20%	53.40%	3.51%	5.63%
Hispanic	12.50%	45.70%	8.93%	19.54%
Total	98.70%	Minority %	21.78%	45.11%

Table 1.14 2020 Micropolitical Demographics and Ownership

Race	% of Population	Ownership Rate	% of Owners Chamber	% of Non-Owners Chamber
White	64.25%	73.20%	74.54%	49.10%
Black	12.80%	41.50%	8.42%	19.03%
Asian	57.00%	53.40%	4.82%	7.36%
Hispanic	16.30%	47.30%	12.22%	24.51%
Total	98.70%	Minority %	25.46%	50.90%

The 1st 3 quarters of 2019 were used with an estimate for 2020 demographics and 2020 Ownership rates.

Table 1.15 2030 Micropolitical Demographics and Ownership

	% of Population	Ownership Rate	% of Owners Chamber	% of Non- owners Chamber
White	61.3%	73.2%	71.2%	48.8%
Black	13.1%	41.5%	8.7%	22.0%
Asian	6.6%	53.4%	5.6%	8.8%
Hispanic	18.9%	47.3%	14.3%	28.6%
Total	98.7%	Minority %	28.7%	59.5%

2020 Home Ownership rates were used in conjunction with 2030 Demographic estimates

Table 1.17 Macropolitical Binary Partition Home Values

State	Party	Median Value	Chamber	Demographic
Michigan	D	134,900	Lower	13
Pennslyvania	D	161,000	Lower	17
Wisconsin	D	167,200	Lower	8
Illinois	D	185,000	Lower	17
Vermont	D	195,000	Lower	1
New Mexico	D	196,330	Lower	3
West Virginia	R	122,550	Lower	2
Ohio	R	130,000	Lower	16
Oklahoma	R	130,500	Lower	5
Kentucky	R	140,000	Lower	6
Alabama	R	143,500	Lower	7
Iowa	R	144,300	Lower	4
South Dakota	R	144,532	Lower	1
Arkansas	R	145,000	Lower	4
Tennesssee	R	145,000	Lower	9
Nebraska	R	152,000	Lower	3
Kansas	R	157,938	Lower	4
Missouri	R	159,668	Lower	8
South Carolina	R	161,500	Lower	7
Louisiana	R	162,000	Lower	6
Indiana	R	163,233	Lower	9
Georgia	R	166,900	Lower	14
North Carolina	R	177,000	Lower	14
Florida	R	185,000	Lower	28
North Dakota	R	190,000	Lower	1
Mississippi	R	207,783	Lower	4
Arizona	R	209,000	6 Lower 3 Upper	9
Idaho	R	210,489	Upper	2
Delaware	D	212,000	Upper	1
Texas	R	214,763	Upper	38
Nevada	D	216,000	Upper	4
Minnesota	D	219,900	Upper	7
Connecticut	D	227,500	Upper	5
Rhode Island	D	230,000	Upper	1
New Hampsire	D	232,000	Upper	2
Maine	D	235,220	Upper	2
Maryland	D	242,000	Upper	8
New York	D	247,000	Upper	27
New Jersey	D	265,000	Upper	12
Oregon	D	275,000	Upper	6
Washington	D	299,000	Upper	10
Colorado	D	300,000	Upper	7
Massachusetts	D	339,900	Upper	9
California	D	422,500	Upper	53
Hawaii	D	485,000	Upper	2
Wyoming	R	219,450	Upper	1
Montana	R	230,608	Upper	1
Utah	R	258,665	Upper	4
Alaska	R	291,530	Upper	1
Virginia	R	297,000	Upper	11

Table 1.18 Southern Reconstruction – Owners Chamber

State	White	AA	AIAIN	ASIAN	Hispanic	% Total	% Loss in Rep
Alabama	76.5%	18.0%	0.6%	1.4%	3.5%	23.5%	10.1%
Mississippi	70.1%	25.8%	0.5%	1.0%	2.6%	29.9%	13.0%
South Carolina	75.1%	18.3%	0.4%	1.7%	4.6%	24.9%	10.4%
North Carolina	73.2%	15.0%	1.3%	3.0%	7.5%	26.8%	10.0%
Georgia	67.5%	21.0%	0.4%	3.9%	7.2%	32.5%	14.9%
Tennessee	82.6%	11.0%	0.4%	1.8%	4.2%	17.4%	7.9%
Florida	64.3%	11.7%	0.4%	2.9%	20.7%	35.7%	11.1%
Arkansas	81.7%	10.2%	0.8%	1.5%	5.7%	18.3%	7.9%
Texas	52.1%	9.4%	0.9%	5.2%	32.5%	47.9%	10.9%
Missouri	87.0%	7.5%	0.5%	1.9%	3.1%	13.0%	6.0%
Kentucky	90.5%	5.3%	0.2%	1.4%	2.7%	9.5%	4.8%
Oklahoma	76.4%	5.3%	7.7%	2.2%	8.5%	23.6%	7.1%

Table 1.19 – Southern Reconstruction – Non-owners chamber

State	White	AA	AIAIN	ASIAN	Hispanic	% Total	% Gain in Rep
Alabama	48.0%	42.7%	0.9%	1.7%	6.6%	52.0%	18.4%
Mississippi	39.2%	54.4%	0.7%	1.2%	4.4%	60.8%	17.9%
South Carolina	46.2%	42.5%	0.7%	2.1%	8.6%	53.8%	18.5%
North Carolina	45.1%	35.0%	2.1%	3.7%	14.0%	54.9%	18.1%
Georgia	38.0%	44.7%	0.6%	4.4%	12.3%	62.0%	14.6%
Tennessee	58.4%	29.5%	0.7%	2.5%	8.9%	41.6%	16.3%
Florida	36.1%	24.9%	0.6%	3.2%	35.2%	63.9%	17.1%
Arkansas	57.2%	27.0%	1.5%	2.1%	12.2%	42.8%	16.6%
Texas	26.2%	17.8%	1.2%	5.2%	49.6%	73.8%	15.0%
Missouri	67.1%	21.7%	0.9%	3.0%	7.3%	32.9%	13.9%
Kentucky	74.2%	16.3%	0.5%	2.2%	6.8%	25.8%	11.5%
Oklahoma	52.1%	13.5%	13.9%	3.0%	17.5%	47.9%	17.2%

ABOUT THE AUTHOR

Jordan David Weisinger graduated from the Johns Hopkins University with a M.S. in Data Analytics (2019), Northwestern University with a M.A. in Public Policy and Administration (2017), and the University of Massachusetts Amherst with a M.B.A in General Management (2015). His undergraduate degree is in Literature from the University of Delaware (2000). Jordan is currently employed as a Business Analyst and spends his days debugging proprietary software for a public organization. Debugging entails breaking software in order to diagnose the defect and repair it. When the quality of a nations leadership and laws are in question, institutional protests are used to break the system in order to cure a defect in leadership or law, to form a more perfect union, in a process identical to debugging.